IN SEARCH
OF THE
GREEN

HOW TO FORM YOUR OWN INVESTMENT CLUB
WHEN YOU DON'T KNOW FROM BEANS

IN SEARCH
OF
THE
GREEN

How To Form Your Own Investment Club When You Don't Know From Beans

By: Patricia E. Edwards, Lisa-René Charles, Mary Ellen Pryor
of the Beanstalk Investment Club of Miami

authorHOUSE™

1663 LIBERTY DRIVE, SUITE 200
BLOOMINGTON, INDIANA 47403
(800) 839-8640
WWW.AUTHORHOUSE.COM

DEDICATION

For my beloved children, Gordon and Dory, and to all the Beanstalk members—past and present—and to those who guided and supported us; my late husband, Dr. Keith D. Edwards, who inspired and believed in me always and to the future generation of investors.

Patricia Edwards

CONTENTS

FOREWORD

Just about 20 years ago, a client invited me to speak to a group of his employees about money and how important it is to prepare for the future. It seemed to have been the first time this group of young women, nurses and nurses aides, stopped to hear about saving, investing, and how anyone can and must do it to protect their future. They were pretty much running to stay in place at the time, balancing kids, careers and, in some cases, marriages. Money issues were foreign to them, except how to make a dollar stretch. But they listened! I'd love to think that a tiny spark that day contributed to these fabulous women creating The Beanstalk Investment Club. But fabulous is the operative word here, and that's just what the Beanstalk ladies are.

Investment clubs are one of the best ways to become "friends" with your finances. Many people don't take the time to pay attention due to intimidation, time constraints, and lack of a "need to know" attitude. Besides, how do you even get started? One of the founders of The Beanstalk Investment Club, Patricia Edwards, recognized that she needed to learn a lot and needed some fun in her life as well, so she, along with Deborah Carattini, and Mary Ellen Pryor, set out to combine the two in an investment club. The rest is history!

To any readers thinking of starting their own investment club or improving an existing one, read on and see how these energetic and smart women created theirs. Learn from their mistakes, as well as their successes. They really know from experience how to do it right, and will help you avoid all the aggravations a new venture can bring.

Follow their example, and follow their lead. It will take you to a place where you can grow and learn, improve your finances, empower yourself, make some close friends, and above all, have fun.

I wish all the readers of this book as much success as the Beanstalk Ladies have had, and as much fun!

To the very special Beanstalk Ladies . . . I'm proud of you, happy for you, and wish you all the successes imaginable!!!

Meg Green, CFP
Meg Green & Associates
North Miami Beach, Florida

ACKNOWLEDGMENTS

We can't say enough about Walt Zawislak, of the now disolved brokerage firm of Quick & Reilly. From day one, he treated us wonderfully and was caught up in our enthusiasm, our innocence, and our schoolgirl naïveté.

We offer special thanks to Phil Keating, CFA, who taught us, and continues to teach us so much through his yearly NAIC sponsored Portfolio Management Workshops.

We also wish to thank Meg Green, CFP, who is a supporter and fan of our club; Abe Bailey, Attorney at Law, who graced our annual meetings; and Harold Hancock, CPA, who advised us in those early days.

We are most appreciative of the support of Marilynn Bever, Mary K. Hesson, Chris Roerden, Ellis Traub, Stacey Bonella, Cynthia and Camille Taylor, and Ruby and Alexandra Grant, whose hard work and encouragement really affirmed our belief in this project. My daughter Dory, thank you for moving the book forward when it seemed hopelessly stalled. My son Gordon, for always being my perpetual cheerleader.

Mary Ellen Pryor, a detail-oriented, tenacious, and loyal friend – thank you is not nearly enough. We co-founded Beanstalk, and without your enthusiasm and shared partnership in creating this book it would not have been the labor of love it turned out to be.

Without my niece Lisa Charles' rigorous word processing skills and unselfish contribution to this effort there might never have been a book. Lisa, I thank you with profound humility.

Lynn Morrow, who designed our cover and retrieved our lost book can only be described as a revivalist. Thank you.

We must thank our families, friends, and all interested, and interesting people we have met since we started the club; each of you has taught us so much.

Finally we thank each other, because we have developed into a great support group. We continue to look forward to our meetings, to learn, and to have fun.

We are as enthusiastic as ever!

IN SEARCH OF THE GREEN: A TRUE FABLE

by Lisa-René Charles

In 1993, a group of courageous women set out on a journey to discover the treasures of untold wealth. Their journey took them to new uncharted territory, and they came upon the Great Verde Pyramid. As they entered the ancient tomb, upon the walls they encountered unfamiliar hieroglyphics: P/E and Beta. Yet one universal symbol, $, assured them they had found the place they were seeking. Through dim passageways, long and narrow, they persevered, taking notes, steadfast in their determination to solve the hieroglyphics. As they penetrated deeper into the tomb they saw a glow at the end of one tunnel. Hurrying toward what they assumed to be the treasure, they came upon a small room. A breeze stirred around them, a swirl of dust appeared, and a gentle voice said unto them, **"Learn to Earn, Learn to Earn, Learn to Earn."** Startled, they looked around but saw no one. Then one of the women noticed a beam of light shining on a hollow in the stone wall. Reaching in, she extracted the Investors Manual of the National Association of Investors Corporation, (NAIC - now known as BetterInvesting). Flipping through its pages, the women saw the symbols they had been looking at throughout their journey and realized they had found the key to deciphering the messages that would surely lead them to their fortunes. Happier and more secure in this newfound knowledge, they retraced their steps to the beginning to learn what each of the symbols on the walls of the great pyramid had to teach them.

Read on, as we share with you the **adventure of starting an investment club.**

PART
I

HOW TO PUT YOUR
INVESTMENT
CLUB TOGETHER

CHAPTER 1

INTRODUCTION TO INVESTMENT CLUBS

In This Chapter
- Why You Need This Guide
- What is an Investment Club
- What is NAIC

The "True Fable," written by the youngest member of our club, Lisa Charles, appeared on the cover of the Annual Report of our Sixth Annual General Meeting. It tells exactly how we felt when we started out. We were eager, but uninformed. Finding the National Association of Investors Corporation (NAIC) manual was a beacon that guided our incredible never-ending journey of successful investing. At this writing, we have been on the Learn to Earn track for the past fourteen years. This is a long time in the life of an investment club. We are proud of being together, and still having fun learning and earning after all these years. You can do it too!

The guidelines presented can be used anywhere in the world to help form an investment club, however, the technical, taxation, and legal requirements such as fictitious name registration, tax identification numbers, and tax filing would need to be researched by the group for your particular country.

Why You Need This *Guide*

In Search of the Green was written to answer the not-so-obvious things you need to know. It is your practical "how to get started without all that frustration and blundering." It is nothing less, and may become a little more, as you Learn to Earn.

In Search of the Green is organized into 18 chapters which guide you through the **why, what, who, where, and how** of successfully starting your investment club. We give you detailed meeting guidelines: checklists, with items that need to be accomplished before, during, and after these organizational meetings. Follow them and you should have a club organized after seven meetings. Not all activities on the checklists have to be done in the exact order presented, nor do you need to get frustrated if all activities are not accomplished as presented, but try to stick as close to the guide as is realistic. Remember, you are in this to learn, to have fun, and to make money. We share some of our errors and some of our successes, and give tips on resources that will not only help you study to buy that first stock, but will also form a foundation for helping your club maintain focus and be a club which is together for many, many years.

We are of the firm belief that, as in most things, if the fundamentals and the foundation are sound at the beginning, and done well, your club will be a sustainable and profitable venture.

This *Guide* is for all the people who want to learn about money in an investment club setting, and who want to invest a little money each month, take a shared risk, and have fun learning together in a group. If this describes your group, this book is for you.

Listen to the mountain climber telling you that it is not difficult to climb Mt. Everest. No problem at all. Just get those boots, the warm gear, the map, and get to that mountain. Right! Or how about the nurse telling you to give an injection and saying it's so easy. Just get the needle, syringe, antiseptic and give the shot. Sure!

Having the gear and the equipment does not mean you are prepared for the task. It is true of human nature that when someone has mastered something he or she often cannot understand why others do not know how to do what now seems so simple—in this case, starting an investment club. Money gurus, or those who are already schooled in investing, no doubt have a clear understanding about stocks and the stock market. For those of you who have no background in the world of investing, we want to take the "mountain climber" and the "nurse" types out of the picture.

Starting an investment club has nothing to do with how smart you are, or how much money you have. Beanstalk members have spoken to many groups over the years and given answers to the questions we address in this book to judges, lawyers, school principals, teachers, insurance adjusters, fast food restaurant workers, scientists, psychologists, retired persons, and business people, young and not so young.

You need instructions, practice, and the opportunity to ask questions. We believe that there are a lot of questions that need to be asked and answered before you begin. *In Search of the Green: How to Form Your Own Investment Club When You Don't Know From Beans* contains the answers to the questions listed below and many others.

- What is an Investment Club?
- How do we find members?
- Why form an Investment club?
- How do we decide on monthly investment dues?
- Do we need an attorney and/or an accountant?
- How do we handle problems – such as members not attending meetings or not paying dues or not participating?
- What do we do when a member wants to leave the club and take his/her money out?
- How often do we meet?
- How do we find a broker?
- What do we do if a member dies?

What Is an Investment Club?

Let us first define what an investment club is. The United States Securities and Exchange Commission website, http://www.sec.gov explains it this way:

"An investment club is a group of people who pool their money to make investments. Usually, investment clubs are organized as partnerships and, after the members study different investments, the group decides to buy or sell based on a majority vote of the members. Club meetings may be educational and each member may actively participate in investment decisions."

We would define an investment club in much the same way, but would say that it is a group of people who pool their money to study and to learn in a systematic manner how to assess companies in order to invest by buying stock in these companies. All club meetings are educational, and for each member to benefit from the investment club experience each one must actively participate in the learning, as well as in the investment decisions.

The business structure of an investment club may take on different forms; however the most typical forms are Partnerships. Beanstalk is organized as a Partnership.

What Is NAIC?

NAIC is the National Association of Investors Corporation, a non-profit volunteer investment educational organization. It is dedicated to increasing the ownership of common stock, by using time-tested stock study tools and methods to teach individuals, as well as investment clubs, how to make educated investment decisions.

NAIC is the leading authority on investment clubs in America, and since 1951, has been helping people learn to invest through the vehicle of investment clubs. Because NAIC is dedicated to developing educational resources to guide and help clubs and individuals invest, your club needs to become a member right away, so put the process in motion. There are other organizations for the individual investor to join and some new ones are emerging to attract investment clubs, but NAIC has stood the test of time. When Beanstalk started we did not join NAIC immediately, and it is not a prerequisite, but it is highly recommended. Why reinvent the wheel? In hindsight, Beanstalk's decision not to join NAIC at the start was not wise. Because NAIC is an established organization, you become a part of a legitimate, time-proven organization of investment clubs, not only in the United States, but all over the world.

Made up primarily of a volunteer staff, the NAIC has provided guidance for investors for more than 50 years. It has developed both manual and computerized tools to help you learn in a systematic way how to analyze companies when buying and selling stocks, as well as mutual funds. NAIC is a resource for training, literature, computer software, and conferences to support your efforts. Each fall it holds a Better Investing National Conference, and every four years an international one. In addition, there are separate regional and national computer conferences. Other resources for monthly local events and workshops are the NAIC Regional Chapters, which are groups that provide support to investment clubs in their respective regions and communities throughout the United States.

NAIC will be a primary source as you establish your club, but be patient if it takes some time to get your material from the essentially volunteer-run organization. To expedite the ordering process you can go to their website. We have had great success placing and receiving orders in a timely manner when using the website. Order the NAIC Official Guide and Membership Guide. You can contact the organization toll free by phone: 1-877-ASK-NAIC, 1-877-275-6242 or by mail: NAIC, P.O. Box 220, Royal Oak, Michigan 48068, or on the web: http://www.better-investing.org and email: service@betterinvesting.org.

There is a cost for clubs to join the NAIC: a fee for the club and a fee for each club member. The fee includes the NAIC's monthly magazine *Better Investing*, for each dues-paying member and one copy of the NAIC Official Guide, plus NAIC Chapter support, member benefits, discount books and computer software, as well as a newsletter for your area's events and educational workshops.

Join NAIC: Initially we were not members of the National Association of Investors Corporation (NAIC), as we did not truly grasp what this organization was all about. Fortunately, for us we became members by January 1992.

As of April 2005, NAIC officially became known as Better Investing.

CHAPTER 2

RECRUITING MEMBERS

*The level of commitment of each member
will determine the character and ultimate success of your club.*

In This Chapter
- The Role of the Founding Members
- Who Can Be a Club Member
- Where Members Live
- Key Questions To Ask About Prospective Members

The single most important decision that will be made is the decision about who should become a club member. This point cannot be overstated. Clubs have failed to get off the ground because there was not the right mix. Clubs have failed to open bank accounts, or buy stocks for months after they have formed, because they could not get past personality issues. Finding members is not the same as finding congenial company for having dinner, going to the movies, or playing cards. Members have to be people who can talk about money, who are good listeners, and who do not see money as the sum total of life. MOSTLY there has to be RESPECT for each other.

The Role of the Founding Members

Now that you understand what an Investment club is, you know it is a neat way to enter the stock market. The next step is setting in motion the preparation to start your own club. The people who decide an investment club is needed are the founding members. At an exploratory meeting these core members should establish the goals, objectives and operating and investment philosophy of the proposed club, and move quickly to get the investment club formed. The primary tasks of the core members, which will be addressed in greater detail in later chapters are:

- Gather some basic information on Investment Clubs
- Get a temporary meeting place.
- Set the first meeting date and time at which the new prospective members will be asked to attend.
- Draft an invitation letter and share your idea for forming a club and include time, date, information, and approximate cost to join the club.
- Prepare an application form and a beneficiary form.

The reality is that there will be two or more founding members doing the groundwork to start the process of getting the club to be a functioning investment club. This core group should set some of the initial goals, expectations, and investment philosophy. As recruiting gets underway, use the groundwork laid out as a guide in selecting your potential members.

Two people do not make an investment club. Having said that, do not be trapped by "the more people, the more money to invest syndrome." You will come to learn that the quality of the investment decisions that will be made are far more meaningful than the number of persons in the club. Large numbers of people can make the club unmanageable, especially in the early planning stages. A good number to start with is between 10 and 14 members. If there is a lot of interest, and membership exceeds 25, we recommend that you start another club. It is the quality, not the quantity of the membership that is important. Very large numbers of people do not make decisions readily.

Recruiting Members

You now need a few people, paying regular monthly dues which are pooled and invested; hence taking on a shared risk while learning and having fun. Start sharing your interest and enthusiasm with people you know who seem interested in learning about investments. Think of people who are open-minded, fun-loving, and adventuresome. Remember diversity when seeking out your fellow adventurers. While birds of a feather may flock together, sometimes it is the understated, different one who turns out to be a superstar. Talk to people at work; go through your address book and make phone calls; talk to people with whom you do business. Talk to family, friends, neighbors, and associates in general, the people where you worship, or people who are members of other clubs in which you share membership.

Just as in all unions, the foundation of your club must be built upon the cornerstone of respect, tolerance, trust, and a sense of kinship. It will be very much like a marriage—strangers for the most part getting together to build an investment life and slowly getting to know one another. Like any lasting marriage there will be bumps to overcome along the way.

You can invite anyone to become a member, but do not forget how important it is to develop the right mix. Whether the members are all women, all men, or a combination of both will be the decision of the membership. Again, it is the elements of respect, compromise, flexibility and trust that matter. The club is yours. It belongs to all members, not a select few. Do what works for you.

As a wedding guest list is not a way to fulfill social obligations, neither is the recruiting activity of an investment club. If you cannot get along with someone outside of the investment club, the odds of both of you getting along within a club are not very good. Maybe you won't ask your spouse, parent, sister, brother, business partner, best friend, or in-law to be part of the club, because his or her personality may not be the right one for the investment club.

Reviews of club portfolios, and studies conducted by NAIC over the years, have shown that clubs made up of a mix of men and women do better than all-female clubs or all-male clubs. However, all-female clubs do better than all-male clubs. Some investment clubs include children. For U.S. clubs, information from the NAIC website suggests that you use the Uniform Gift/Transfer to Minors Act, (UGMA/UTMA), in effect in your state, with a parent or other adult as custodian. There are all-children clubs that are sponsored by an adult who gives guidance and makes the trades on behalf of the club. Any children in clubs have to work in the club at learning like everyone else. NAIC and a number of websites on the Internet have developed excellent tools to help children understand and learn about investing and the value of money. Some schools are even forming investment clubs for the children.

Where Members Live

Be creative in finding your members. In this age of technology, a number of clubs have members who live all over the United States and other parts of the world. They conduct meetings via the Internet, e-mail, and some even develop web pages. No matter whether your club is an old fashioned, face-to-face, breathing the same air in the same room club, or you are in cyberspace, the message of selecting the right mix still holds.

Whether members live in one community or state will be a critical factor. Based on the objectives of your club and whether you are a computer-operated club or a face-to-face club, where your members live is important. Beanstalk recruited all over the country, and with many out-of-town members, the task of preparing and presenting education topics at meetings fell to a small core of local members. While there are still a few out-of-area and out-of-state members, to increase participation, we revised our by-laws. Now new members must live in the Tri-county area; this means no one is more than an hour's drive from any meeting place. Out-of-town members maintain contact through e-mail, or attend meetings via speaker phone on occasion. Taking full advantage of the benefits of being a club member is difficult when people are far away. Remember, be creative. If you don't have e-mail, contributing to a club newsletter by regular mail may work for you.

Key Questions To Ask About Prospective Members

When thinking about potential people to ask to join the club, ask yourself the following questions:

1. What is the right mix for the club - all women, all men, all children, or some combination of these groups?
2. Do they share the same investment philosophy you intend to establish for your club?
3. Do they believe in investing for the long term, or are they more the buy low, sell high, get rich quick personality type?
4. How do they describe themselves in terms of risk taking?:

   • High risk-speculator
   • Moderate risk-aggressive

- Long term growth-conservative
- Some combination of these

5. Do they see the club as a way to make a lot of money quickly?
6. Do they see the club as an educational opportunity to learn about stocks and investing?
7. Do they have the work ethic to be ongoing contributing members to the club's continued learning and earning goals?
8. Do they see that down the road they may transform this knowledge into improving their personal financial future?
9. What interests, unique qualities, or strengths will each person bring to the club?
10. How will each person fit in with the the group? Is he/she a leader, follower, dictator, mediator, facilitator, mentor, educator?
11. Do they like to have fun? Are they enthusiastic, and ready to go for it?
12. Have they really given much thought to many of these questions?

These questions are listed here to help guide your thinking about whom to invite to become members. It is not a test, or an interview questionnaire.

• Change is the law of life, and those who look only to the past or present are certain to miss the future.
JOHN F. KENNEDY

• Aim for success, not perfection. Never give up your right to be wrong, because then you will lose the ability to learn new things and to move forward in your life.
DR. DAVID BURNS

How important is Membership Participation?

The material presented in this section on membership participation is adapted from the NAIC website topic, <u>Investment Clubs and the Securities and Exchange Commission (SEC)</u>. It is presented for general information purposes only, and is not to be considered legal advice from either the authors or NAIC.

Questions regarding applicability of this information to your specific circumstances should be directed to an attorney with experience in securities law or the appropriate governmental agency.

You may be wondering about some of the following questions:

- Can an investment club recruit new members through advertising?
- Should a club retain members who have become inactive?
- In order to have more money to invest, should a club accept new members who won't participate in club activities?
- How can a club determine if it is making a public offering of a security that must be registered?

The answers to these questions are not merely club policy, but may have legal implications.

NAIC discourages the use of advertising by investment clubs to attract new members, primarily because advertising for members may result in violations of federal and state securities laws. A club that offers memberships through mass media advertising, or postings on the Internet is making a public offering, not a private placement. The SEC recognizes that investment clubs usually are not subject to regulation under the securities laws. However, their policy statement warns that there are circumstances where offering a membership in an investment club may require registration under the Federal Securities Act.

Simply forming a club as a general partnership will not guarantee that a club complies with the securities laws. The SEC and state administrators will review each situation on a case-by-case basis, but the reality may be that a club with inactive members has, in fact, issued securities to them. If some club members do not actively participate in the business of the club, then these members are, in effect, expecting to profit from the investment management provided by the active members. If you are the custodian of an all-children club, to avoid passive member problems with the SEC, the custodian should be allowed to vote.

So the question is, "Are a club's membership interests securities?" The Supreme Court has said that a security, which encompasses more than the stocks and bonds we typically recognize as securities, exists if the following three elements are present:

1. An investment
2. A common enterprise
3. Profits derived solely from the efforts of others

While all investment club memberships have the first two characteristics, what distinguishes an investment club is that it usually does not have the third. According to the SEC:

"If every member in an investment club actively participates in deciding what investments to make, the membership interests in the club would probably not be considered securities. If the club has passive members, it may be issuing securities."

Investment clubs are not mutual funds. But the more a club looks and acts like a mutual fund, the more likely it is to be subjected to regulation by the SEC and state securities agencies.

As noted by NAIC and the SEC, education is the primary objective of most investment clubs. Clubs that carefully recruit, screen and train new members to ensure that they are genuinely interested in learning to become better investors and that they take steps to ensure the active participation of members in club activities, should have little difficulty establishing that their membership interests are not securities.

CHAPTER 3

SETTING UP THE CLUB STRUCTURE

IN THIS CHAPTER
- Choosing the Legal Structure
- Naming the Club
- Is it necessary to have an Attorney and an Accountant
- Electing Officers

As you are organizing the formal structure of your investment club, there are actions that are going to be undertaken as you meet. The topics covered in this chapter are tasks that will require possibly months of work before they are completed. We tell you this up front so that you don't get panicked by thinking you must have these items set in stone before you can begin forming your club. To complete these tasks you will need the participation and feedback of your fellow club members, but we present the information to you now so that you, the founding members, will include these areas in your groundwork for starting your club.

Choosing the Legal Structure

While a club may take the form of any legal entity, most clubs choose to become partnerships. Generally, investment clubs are not organized as corporations so as to avoid double taxation of the club and the individual members. As making a profit is one of the primary objectives of an investment club, and a member's share of those profits is subject to individual federal and state taxes, a club cannot be formed as a non-profit organization for taxation purposes.

As outlined in the manual of the National Association of Investors Corporation, a partnership is defined as follows: "An association of two or more persons to carry on as co-owners of a business for profit." When the partnership is established, a formal document called a Partnership Agreement is prepared and signed by all partners. Included in the NAIC manual is a sample Partnership Agreement that addresses how the club will operate. Included in the Appendix of this *Guide* is a copy of Beanstalk's Agreement. You may adapt these resources to the needs of your club.

Make sure each club member has carefully read the agreement and agrees to abide by these club rules. Whenever a change in your membership occurs, you should amend your Partnership Agreement by preparing a revised agreement and securing each member's signature. If this is logistically impractical, (say you decided to have out of state members), you may send the signature page of the partnership agreement to the member. By signing the member agrees to abide by the agreement. Then at a follow up meeting or the Annual Meeting, present the revised Partnership Agreement for all members to sign.

The Partnership Agreement is not something you are likely to have finished in the first seven organizational meetings, but once you have started and established yourselves as a group try to get it completed and signed as quickly as possible.

Naming the Club

The next two crucial steps needed to form the legal structure of the club are the following:

1. Filing for a Fictitious Name
2. Obtaining a Tax Identification Number

A fictitious name is the term applied to the name chosen for a formal partnership. As a partnership you require a name. Be creative; ask for suggestions when naming your club. Keep in mind that you want your name to reflect your objective. Have fun doing this. Let the imagination explode.

Registration requirements may vary from state to state; therefore, to protect the chosen name of your partnership, contact your County

Clerk's Office. Generally the Fictitious Name registration and fee renewal are due after 10 years. You may also be required to publish your chosen name in the newspapers. Here are the steps we followed in the state of Florida to get the fictitious name the BEANSTALK Investment Club of Miami.

- Have your proposed investment club's name ready. Choose a back-up name just in case the name you picked has already been used. In some communities the name verification, (did someone else use that name already), can be done over the phone.
- Call your local community newspaper, (the rates are cheaper than for a city daily), and explain that you want to advertise a fictitious name. They will quote the advertising rate (and in most cases supply the form) and walk you through any additional steps. If your city only has one paper, then that is the paper you will have to use.
- Complete the form, pay the money required to advertise it, and any filing fees. Check that the name has appeared in the paper the designated number of times, (buy the paper and look for the name), and call the newspaper after the time frame it gave you. If no one has claimed the name then YOUR CLUB HAS A NAME! YOU REALLY HAVE BEGUN! We were so excited at this point.

The next step is getting a TAX ID number. Look in the telephone book for your nearest IRS office and apply over the phone to obtain your TAX/EIN (Employer Identificaion Number) instantly. You can also request that the IRS mail the application form to you. Once it arrives, complete and return it either by mail or via fax as instructed by the IRS. This form is also known as the SS-4 and can be downloaded from the Internet at http://www.irs.gov. (Sample of form in Appendix)

Your Tax ID number, or EIN, is like a Social Security number for your partnership. This is the number under which the IRS tracks each member's profits and losses on his/her club investment when each one files his individual tax return each year. Do not let this frighten you. The person with the most work around income tax time is the Treasurer, and the NAIC Club Accounting program is set up to make it all very manageable.

Is it Necessary to Have an Attorney or Accountant?

Because there are formal agreements and money involved, immediately thoughts turn to whether hiring an attorney or an accountant is necessary to advise and help set up the club.

We found that it was not necessary to hire the services of an Attorney or an Accountant to set up the club; however, if the founding members, or the club membership wish to discuss any concerns with a professional, then do so.

There is no need for an attorney to be involved in the ongoing operations of the club. Being an attorney and being an investment club member are two different things. In our visits to other clubs to tell them how to start a club, the attorneys were asking the same questions we are sharing with you throughout this *Guide*.

A certified public accountant is also not necessary for the ongoing operation of the club. If you have a friend who is an accountant, and you want to review the tax implications and filing requirements of the chosen business structure with a professional accountant, that's ok. It's your option to choose to do so or not.

Try to keep in mind that this is a simple investment club, and it is not necessary to pay for the services of a lawyer and an accountant to set up the club. The Partnership Agreement and the club operations are not complicated, and with the support and participation of the club members, you can do it yourselves.

Let us tell you a story. Neither of our two best treasurers knew anything about accounting. One of them, Francene Simmonds, a young member of Beanstalk, took on the job in our early years when we used pen and paper accounting. She did not like numbers and thought she could not do the job. The club assured her they thought she could do it, and do it well. She painstakingly learned the NAIC club accounting method and was so superb that she was our treasurer for three years, and has again assumed that position after getting a break for several years.

It is recommended that you purchase the NAIC Club Accounting computer software designed for Investment Clubs. Beanstalk uses the NAIC Club Accounting software, which is constantly updated, and which has a special program to help the treasurer file the tax reporting to the Internal Revenue Service each year. Managing the club's accounts does take time, and the person needs to be detail-oriented, patient, have the time to update records, make stock purchases, and execute the club's financial transactions in a timely, accurate and organized fashion.

Electing Officers

From among the founding members, designate a leader or president-elect, secretary-elect and treasurer-elect until the club is formed and elections are held for each of these offices. Don't get territorial; let people who are willing to try and are able to take on elected positions and other key roles do so. No one owns the club. Each one of you is a partner. The actual founding member of Beanstalk was not elected to be its first president, and never has been the president. What is best for the club must override all other personality issues. Beanstalk suggests the following elected and non-elected positions:

Elected	*Role*
President	presides over the monthly meetings
Vice-President	substitutes for president, if absent
Treasurer	responsible for all club accounting
Assistant Treasurer	substitutes for treasurer, as needed
Secretary	maintains minutes / club correspondence

Non-Elected Positions	*Role*
Education Committee	presents education topics at monthly meetings
Historian	keeps record of all printed material about club
Parliamentarian	assists the president in keeping order, if needed
Social Chair/Hospitality	sends cards/flowers for appropriate occasions

In Beanstalk, elections are held once per year at the Annual General Meeting. We used to elect new officers each year, but found that just as they were getting comfortable with the role and responsibilities, a new person was elected. Beanstalk now holds elections for the positions of president and vice-president on an annual basis, but every two years for the positions of treasurer and secretary. This works well for the club because the process of getting new bank signatures does not have to be done each year. It also provides continuity, allowing understudies to get a chance to really learn the positions. The position of club secretary needs someone who is willing to take minutes and handle correspondence. The club may also need someone who has access to a computer and knows how to use it, or is willing to learn.

As you can see, the positions of President or Presiding Partner, Vice-President or Assistant Presiding Partner, Secretary or Recording Partner and Treasurer or Financial Partner are some of the key positions in the club. Use these traditional titles or make up some fun titles of your own. The club needs leadership and direction.

If people accept positions, they must be held accountable. This does not mean that the rest of the members just sit back and do nothing. Club officers need to spread the tasks around to all members. Delegation, Participation, Cooperation—these elements are key to the success of any club. The club needs EVERYBODY, but unless all of you know what each of the others can do, or likes to do, or would like to try to do, you may miss out on some of your own best resources.

Motivating those with whom you work often is as simple as giving them a sense of purpose and belonging.

UNKNOWN

Ability is what you do ...
Motivation determines what you do ...
Attitude determines how well you do it.

UNKNOWN

CHAPTER 4

Forms You Will Need

In This Chapter
- Application/Beneficiary Form
- Meeting Agenda
- Meeting Minutes
- Treasurer's Report
- Bylaws

So far we have focused on what an investment club is, how to recruit members, and how to become a legal entity. In this chapter we will give you some tips for creating forms and bylaws that will help you avoid unforeseen problems. Samples of these forms are included in the Appendix.

Application/Beneficiary Form

It is a good idea to have each member complete an application form, giving basic information needed for ease in communication and for completing year-end tax forms. This information should include: name, address, phone, fax, e-mail, and social security number. The application should also contain an area where club members can name their beneficiaries. This is necessary should someone in the club die. Unfortunately, this can happen, and it did in our first year. When a founding member died, it was expedient to have her wishes on paper.

Meeting Agenda

We strongly advise that an agenda be prepared for each meeting. The agenda will help to keep your meetings on track and within the allotted time frame. Here is a simple sample Meeting Agenda for your club - The Early Years.

Your Club Name

Meeting Agenda

Date

Call to Order

Approve Minutes

Treasurer's Report

Pay Dues

Old Business

Education

Stock Study

Stock Purchase

Next Meeting

Stocks to Study next meeting

Adjournment

Under each heading you can place any additional information you feel is pertinent, and of course, you should adapt this example to suit your needs. One additional tip: we found it very helpful to indicate on the agenda to whom checks for dues should be made payable.

Meeting Minutes

There has to be a record of what takes place during the meetings. You need to make note of all decisions made. Beanstalk now takes minutes by keeping a cassette recorder on during meetings. The tape is then transcribed and minutes are distributed by the club secretary. A tape recorder is especially helpful if you are not experienced with taking notes and participating in a meeting at the same time. Keep copies of the minutes in a permanent file, and have the secretary bring one complete set of all minutes to each meeting for reference. Copies of the prior meeting's minutes should be distributed to each club member to review and approve. From your first organizational meeting, start a meeting minutes binder and store it by month and year.

Treasurer's Report

At each meeting the treasurer should give a report stating the balances in all bank and money market accounts, any outstanding dues, any reimbursements or distributions made on behalf of the club, and any stocks purchased or sold. This information will become a part of the minutes. If you are using the NAIC Club Accounting computer program, the treasurer will also be able to provide the club with a portfolio valuation, as well as individual member valuation statements.

Bylaws

There are written rules which the club itself develops. These are called Bylaws. They are the detailed and specific rules that govern your club's conduct. They are really simple sentences—keep them simple—that determine what the club will do in any given set of circumstances. For example, they should address the maximum number of members the club will allow; include what educational seminars future members will need to attend before joining the club; state how members join ("buy in") and how members leave the club; what percentage of the club's holdings a member may not exceed; and specify the length of service for elected club officers.

If there is someone who has experience with preparing bylaws, let him or her go for it. Just be sure the bylaws reflect what the club members agreed upon. Or in the beginning, you can do what Beanstalk did: get a copy of the bylaws from another organization and adjust them to suit your needs until members get a better understanding of the club's operating procedures. As the club grows, you will determine how and when bylaws need to be amended to reflect the individuality of your club. In the Appendix, we have included a sample of Beanstalk's current bylaws. They have changed a lot from our first year, as yours, no doubt, will.

After Beanstalk had been operating for a couple of years, and we had more knowledge and confidence, we established a bylaws committee to review and propose amendments to our bylaws. We now try to limit amendments to the bylaws to once a year at our Annual General Meeting.

Bylaws help solve people problems. Everything is not going to go without problems. Because we are people, people problems do occur. Right in the beginning, you may observe that there are members who do not come to meetings or pay their dues. While you are organizing the club, address this problem immediately because these people will affect the club's morale and the amount of funds available to invest, and are probably ones who should not continue as members of the club. In your bylaws, specifically state how these problems will be handled. For example, the bylaws may state how many missed meetings constitute a potential for removal from the club, as well as procedures for removal. The club may require written notice if a club member knows he/she is going to miss several meetings and expect the monthly investment to be paid on time regardless of the absence. Some clubs charge a penalty fee irrespective of the reason you are not able to attend meetings. Failure to collect your monthly investments in a timely manner should not be a problem if all members attend meetings. However, this problem may arise and therefore, procedures for handling this situation should also be included in your bylaws. Perhaps the club can issue a series of three notices if dues are outstanding over a 90-day period, which state that after notice #3, the individual club member will be removed from the club.

In the bylaws, establish what costs, penalties, or forfeiture periods the club will attach to the withdrawing member. There are many ways to handle this "buy-out" event. Define these procedures clearly in the bylaws. Some clubs "buy out" the member with stock. More often though the club has to sell stock to "buy-out" the member with cash. A formal resignation letter is required by Beanstalk. The post-mark date of the resignation letter is used to determine the member's valuation, (the amount of money she has in the club). This valuation, less any penalties as stated in our bylaws, is the buy-out amount the club owes the member. Additionally, the bylaws of many clubs specify a 90-day lag period between valuation and issue of payment. Hopefully, this will allow time for your club to accumulate cash and avoid having to sell stocks to make the payment.

CHAPTER 5

START UP COSTS

In This Chapter
- Cost for Starting a Club
- Monthly Investment Amount
- Insurance and Taxes Summary
- Finding a Bank
- Finding a Broker

There are costs for starting an investment club. Typically there are start-up costs to cover initial expenditures to get the club started; membership fees for ongoing administrative costs of operating the club, such as postage, copying, annual membership fees to NAIC; and the club members' monthly investment.

Cost for Starting a Club

These are generally one-time fees that can include photocopying costs, money for obtaining the Fictitious Name, computer software, videos, worksheets to do stock analysis and club accounting, plus the membership fee to NAIC. Therefore, figure between $150 and $200 per person (it can be less, it could be a bit more). There is no hard and fast rule for this. Set this fee at a dollar figure that is affordable and also meets the needs of the club.

The decision as to how much money will be needed for start-up costs will depend on:

- How many people are in your club?
- Will you purchase computer software for club accounting?
- Will you purchase computer software to analyze the stocks?
- Will you use the paper and pen method of doing your accounting and stock analysis?
- Will you join NAIC?
- What other miscellaneous organizational expenses do you have?

Beanstalk had a lower start up cost for its members as the founders underwrote some of the initial costs.

Membership Fees/Dues

Each year membership fees will be due to NAIC for both the club and individual members. Collect an annual assessment fee each year from each member to cover NAIC fees and other costs such as the cost of postage, upgrading computer software, educational materials, photocopying or buying new software.

Monthly Investment Fees

The monthly investment fee is very different from the start-up or membership fees. The investment fee is the amount each member is required to bring to the club each month so that stocks can be purchased. This money is to be used exclusively for investments.

The amount of each member's monthly contribution is usually between $20 and $50 dollars. Some clubs have a monthly investment as high as $100 or more, but this is not typical. Over time the monthly investment amount may be adjusted by an amendment to the club's bylaws.

Each time a member makes a monthly investment, that member purchases a unit, or some fraction thereof, of the club. If your club were a company that sold stocks, a unit would be similar to a share of stock. The number of units you own, multiplied by the value of the unit, determines your ownership in the club. At the club's inception the value of one unit is usually equal to the monthly investment fee. As your portfolio grows the value of a unit will fluctuate with the performance of the portfolio.

A member can buy more than one unit at each meeting. In the bylaws you will state the largest percentage of the club portfolio that any member is allowed to own. This will prevent the situation of one member having so much ownership in the club that he or she controls it.

Insurance

Insurance in the form of a Fidelity Bond is available through the NAIC. Alternatively, you can contact your insurance agent and purchase a Fidelity Bond. This is insurance against embezzlement of the club's funds. Beanstalk has never felt the need to have a bond, but we have heard of instances where clubs do have it. This is a decision the club must make. Don't get bogged down in this and let it stop your forward movement of getting the club started.

Taxes

The tax reporting year is from January to December. The club's fiscal year does not need to coincide with the Tax Year. The club is required to submit Form1065, Annual Partnership Return, to the IRS. The club Treasurer is responsible for ensuring that all documents are prepared. The individual club members receive a Schedule K-1 from the Treasurer that shows the worth of each person's investment, and any profit or loss for the year. If the member does not prepare his own taxes, he shows the form to the person who prepares his taxes. This information will be treated on the member's income tax return as either additional income or a loss. This *Guide* does not address taxes in depth. You can learn more about this topic from NAIC's special workshops and *Better Investing* Magazine.

Finding a Bank

So far things are pretty straightforward. Where to keep your money and how to open a bank account for the club can get complicated, if you allow it. There are clubs that did not open a bank account for almost nine months after they were formed because they went to the wrong banks, with the wrong information, or there was controversy as to who should be in charge of the club's money.

Make this simple for yourselves. Go to a commercial bank, with a low or no fee checking account, if you can find one. Credit Unions are changing so they may be more receptive to opening an account for your club. Designate your club's President and Treasurer as the account holders, or two other members who have easy access to the bank for opening a savings account. We are sure that there are those of you who will be reading this that will ask about on-line banking; Beanstalk has never done it, so we cannot offer any information.

Go to the bank, with the Tax ID number, open the account under your club's name and have the signature card signed. Initially we made it a requirement that two signatures were required for withdrawing funds. Over time we found it easier to have two authorized signers, but either person could withdraw funds on the club's behalf. Coordinating the schedules of both signers to withdraw funds became a logistical nightmare. Typically start-up and membership fees are deposited in this checking account. The monthly investment fee can be deposited in this account initially. However a strict accounting has to be kept, as investment money is not to be co-mingled or mixed with other monies. Investment dues are to be used for buying stock. This is an absolute.

The club can open a money market account with the brokerage firm that the club will select to buy and sell stocks. A money market account has check writing privileges, although there may be a minimum amount for which checks can be written. The money market funds can be automatically withdrawn to make the stock purchase if the same brokerage firm is used for the money market account and stock trades. Typically the monthly investment fees are deposited into this account. Use a no fee savings account or a separate checking account for all other monies, such as annual assessment fees and start up costs.

Finding a Broker

There are three main types of brokers: (1) full commission or full service brokers, (2) discount brokers, and (3) on-line brokers.

The full service brokers, such as Merrill Lynch, employ experienced stockbrokers who research companies, analyze stocks, and make suggestions to their customers as to what to buy. They charge a fee, and purchase stocks based on your belief in the information they provide you. The trade-off for this service is the highest commission fees of the three types of brokers.

The discount brokers also employ experienced stockbrokers; however, they do not make suggestions as to what stocks to purchase. As a result the commission fees are significantly lower or *"discounted,"* because the club does the research, not the discount broker. The club Treasurer, or other designated club officer, calls the broker and instructs them to buy stocks in the companies your club agreed upon.

If you are Internet savvy, the cost is lower yet, because you can execute your stock trades on-line. Both full service and discount brokerages are offering low cost per trade options via the Internet. Be careful and make sure you read the fine print to determine if you are getting a better deal.

How do we find a broker that's right for our club?

As Beanstalk was trying to get started, the standard reply to many of our questions was "just call a broker." Remember the mountain climber; it's easy if you know how. First determine the type of broker your club wants to use. Go to the library and look at the financial magazines, such as *Money*, and *Kiplinger*, or look in NAIC's *Better Investing* if you have a copy. All of these publications contain advertisements by brokers. If you have access to the Internet, surf the web. Checkout the broker information and ratings links on the NAIC website in the FAQ's – Investment Clubs section.

Get quotes on the commission charged by both discount and full service brokers and make a comparison. We recommend that you select a discount broker who has no restrictions or minimums, and offers all of the services listed in "Finding a Good Broker" at the end of this chapter. Once you have selected a broker request an application.

Do we always have to buy stock through a broker?

No. More and more the middleman is being replaced. We will just briefly tell you that stocks can be purchased directly from specific companies through Dividend Re-investment Programs, or "DRIPS." NAIC also has a program called the Low Cost Investment Program. If you are a NAIC member, there is a nominal set-up fee to enroll, plus the price of one share of the stock you wish to purchase.

FINDING A GOOD BROKER

Take a few names from the advertisements in the financial magazines, or from the Internet, and call.

How you are treated on the phone is a good indicator of whether the broker wants your business or not.

Ask the following questions:

1. Does the Broker accept Investment Club accounts?
2. Will the Broker allow you to buy one stock?
3. Will the Broker charge you to keep the stock certificates?
4. Do you have to purchase stocks in lots, for example: in groups of 100 shares?
5. Is the Broker's commission for one stock the same as it is for one thousand?
6. Will the Broker assign someone to deal specifically with your club?
7. Does the brokerage firm have a money market account with free checking?
8. If the Broker offers on-line trading, what are the special conditions or restrictions, for example: how often do you have to make an online trade and is there a minimum purchase amount?

If a broker imposes restrictions that penalize you for using or not using online trading, that is not good.

PART II

HOW TO ORGANIZE YOUR FIRST MEETINGS

CHAPTER 6

SELECTING A MEETING PLACE

IN THIS CHAPTER
- Where To Meet
- When To Meet
- How To Meet
- The Investing Cycle

As simple as this sounds, treat the selection of a meeting place with great care, because how you accommodate your club's need for a safe and comfortable atmosphere, where you can get down to business, requires special care. Do not set these decisions aside on a back burner, or leave them until the last minute. Consider the following points when addressing where to meet, when to meet, and how to meet.

Where To Meet

- Is the meeting area centrally located and accessible to club members?
- Is the meeting area free from distractions and interruptions?
- Is the meeting area available for at least 2 hours?

- Will a meal, snack, or beverages be provided?
- Does the meeting area allow food?
- Are there adequate, comfortable seating and writing surfaces for members?
- Are additional resources provided at the meeting area (for example, computer access, a television and VCR, DVD player, or overhead, lap top)?
- Is there a cost for the meeting area or for additional equipment?
- If meeting in club members' homes are all club members willing to host or to feed the members?

Beanstalkers have met in each other's homes for the past 10 years. In looking back we believe that was the right decision for us. It helped solidify the group. Many of us did not know each other, and what better way to get to know each other than over a good meal at the end of the meeting. For the most part we typically do not do things socially as a group, but we are there for each other during a crisis, such as the Hurricane in Miami which completely destroyed the homes of some of our members. We are there during sickness and death, you know like that marriage we talked about earlier. No we don't always agree, and we have had very strong disagreements, but because we respect each other, we can always settle back and continue with our wonderful club.

This may not be how your group wishes to operate. Do what is comfortable. Some clubs meet in church halls, boardrooms, condo meeting rooms, office conference rooms, libraries, or facilities in private businesses which open their meeting rooms to the community free of charge or for a nominal fee. If you have the opportunity to meet in a facility where there are computers, and it is free, safe, and convenient, such a location is worthy of consideration.

In our club, the hosting member serves a meal at the end of each of our meetings. In general, we all like to entertain, so it is done with great care and style, but there was a short period when we actually had to do an informal survey as to whether we would have food. In the beginning it was always understood that if a meal was prepared it should be a low cost meal. That soon went out the window as members cooked their favorite foods and presented the meal in a festive manner. Other clubs serve light refreshments, some serve only coffee, some have no food or drink whatsoever.

When To Meet

- Depends on the availability of the meeting area
- Depends on the availability of members
- Decide on the best day of the week and time of day to hold meetings
- Set a regularly scheduled day and time
- Be sure members commit to the meeting frequency and time
- Be consistent about the meeting schedule; start and end meetings on time and within the time frame agreed upon.

After the initial meetings to form the club, investment clubs typically meet once per month on a specific date or day and at a specific time, (e.g; the 3rd Saturday of the month from 1 to 3 PM). An actual meeting usually lasts between 1 $1/2$ and 2 hours.

How To Meet

- Actively support the four aspects of our cornerstone: Respect, Tolerance, Trust, and Kinship
- Operate the club as you would operate a successful business, and with fun
- Establish meeting ground rules and expectations
- Follow some form of "rules of conduct" for conducting meetings and voting
- Value your time and keep meetings on schedule
- Prepare and distribute a written meeting agenda in advance of the meeting (see Appendix for a sample agenda)
- Don't rush the meeting – focus on club objectives and investment principles
- Make investment education a priority
- Set up ad-hoc meetings to deal with in-depth issues (e.g. partnership agreement content)
- Create subcommittees as needed to support the ongoing operation of the club (e.g. Bylaws, Education or Stock Analysis committees)
- Empower subcommittees to make recommendations to the club
- Keep written records of all meetings and decisions
- Set aside one meeting a year to review prior objectives and to plan for the upcoming year

Although this is not a board meeting of a major company, or the Congress of the United States of America, there needs to be order and rules for conducting the meeting. Not all of us are familiar with the basic rules of conducting a simple meeting. But rules of conduct make the meetings go faster, finish in a timely manner, allow all members to be heard, and more gets accomplished.

While an investment club has a relatively informal meeting atmosphere, it does deal with money, and decisions are made about how money is spent. There is need for order and simple voting procedures. For example, after discussion of a topic if one wants a vote on the topic, make a simple statement outlining what you want to say and present it. This is called making a motion. For the motion to be accepted, the president or parliamentarian restates the motion and another member needs to agree that the statement is accepted by saying so. This is called seconding the motion. If the motion is not seconded then it dies, and no further action is taken. If "seconded," the motion then goes to a vote. All club members are then asked to vote, yes, no or abstain, (not cast a vote at all). In Beanstalk it takes a majority of the votes cast to pass the motion. Beanstalk Bylaws set the number of members in good standing needed to form a quorum, (the number of members required to transact the business of the club), and state that only members in good standing are eligible to vote.

If no one in the club knows parliamentary procedure, but members know how to conduct an orderly gathering, that is a good starting point. While not absolutely necessary, it is useful to have as a reference, a meeting rules book. Get a copy of *Roberts Rules of Order*, but don't go and buy a new one, try a second hand book store or find a used one on the Internet. Remember this is not a "must" have.

The Investing Cycle©

The use of the garden as our method of walking you through starting the club naturally aligns with the imagery of the Beanstalk. Beanstalk members believe in the Harvest Philosophy and practice it through the Investing Cycle. There are seven steps in the Investing Cycle, and in order to reap bountiful harvests you must be an attentive gardener. Bad habits are hard to break, good habits you must cultivate.

THE INVESTING CYCLE ©
7 STEPS TO SUCCESSFUL INVESTING©

1. Choose Your Garden

2. Prepare the Soil

3. Plant the Seeds

4. Divide Your Beds

5. Tend the Crops

6. Pull the Weeds

7. Reap What You Sow

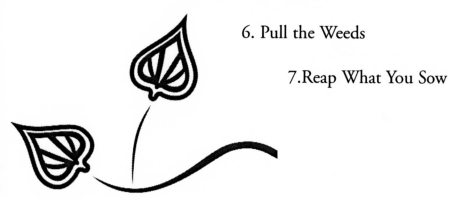

© 2002. The Investing Cycle and the 7 Steps to Successful Investing are Copyrights of the authors.

1. *Choose your Garden*

The garden encompasses the right people and a flexible investment portfolio, so choose your members and your investments wisely.

2. *Prepare the Soil*

Foundation - Participation - Education - Evaluation

Equip yourselves with the tools and knowledge to create a fertile environment for the seeds of your investments to grow. An attentive gardener will reap the best harvests by using the best seeds in properly prepared soil.

3. *Plant the Seeds*

Choose your investments following your club's established principles and objectives. The club will thrive if each member agrees to study and to learn, and actively shares this knowledge by educating others.

4. *Divide your Beds*

All good farmers know that while one crop may be the money maker, it is always prudent to have other crops planted - just in case. So too should you embrace the philosophy of diversification, across several sectors and industries to protect you from fluctuations in the market, as well as diversification in club membership.

5. *Tend the Crops*

Nurture your investments. Keep abreast of what's happening with the companies you have invested in, and what's happening in the marketplace. Invest regularly in your portfolio, as well as in your knowledge base.

6. *Pull the Weeds*

Review your portfolio's performance. Evaluate investments for potential "sells." Don't be afraid to replace poor performers with top-ranked companies in their sector and industry. Review your membership, and don't be afraid to replace uncommitted members with more energized, enthusiastic ones.

7. Reap What You Sow

Watch your club and investments bloom under your vigilant and nurturing care. Decide whether to buy, hold, or replace stocks in your portfolio. When your investments have achieved your club's objectives, evaluate your portfolio for potential liquidation of some appreciation using your defined exit strategy.

Every good farmer knows that if you keep planting the same crops in the same bed, year after year, eventually the harvest diminishes because the soil is overworked. Replenish the soil! Your club, and your portfolio, are dynamic entities. Cultivate your learning and your investments. Continuously follow *The Investing Cycle*. Your destiny is in your hands!

LAW OF THE HARVEST

Sow a thought, reap an action.
Sow an action; reap a habit.
Sow a habit; reap a character.
Sow a character; reap a destiny.

In the next eight chapters we provide detailed guidelines for conducting your organizational meetings, your first club meeting, and your Annual Harvest Meeting. The meeting guidelines are organized into five sections:

The Meeting Objective
1. *Housekeeping Action Items* – to be completed prior to the meeting
2. *Administrative Action Items* – maintenance items to be addressed during the meeting
3. *Operating Action Items* – to determine operating procedures, bylaws or investing principles
4. *Follow-up Action Items* – to be completed before the next meeting

CHAPTER 7

MEETING #1: CHOOSE YOUR GARDEN

Objective of Meeting # 1:

To gather potential club members and information and to begin the process of starting an investment club.

Housekeeping Action Items

- If desired, founding members have met with a lawyer and an accountant.
- Gather basic information on investment clubs.
- Get sample partnership agreement and bylaws.
- Send invitation letter to prospective charter members.
- Prepare an application/beneficiary form.
- Bring open minds.
- Meet in a comfortable place.
- Be sure to set a time limit - 2 to 3 hours.
- Have light refreshments.
- Have pen and paper, and a computer, if available.
- Ask each member to keep all investment club information in a personal binder or folder and bring it to all meetings.
- Buy binders at the outset for the club's use for these things:
  - Minutes
  - Completed application forms and member address lists
  - Treasurer's records
  - Articles and miscellaneous information you will collect
  - Stock Selection Guides and Stock Study Worksheets
- Club Scrapbook - to keep a history of the club.

Administrative Action Items

- Assign someone to take meeting notes.
- Keep organized notes of this meeting and include them in your Meeting Minutes binder.
- Decide on the geographic area from which members will be drawn.
- Complete a contact list of names, addresses, e-mail, and phone numbers.
- Prepare an inventory of "assets" among those present at the meeting, such as, who owns a computer, who likes to write, who likes to teach, who likes figures or is willing to learn, who can get free copying, who can arrange for free convenient meeting places if you are not meeting in members' homes, etc. (See sample Membership Resource List in Appendix.)
- Identify who will call the community newspaper or the local daily paper to get information on advertising for a fictitious name.
- Remind whoever takes on the responsibility of paying any fees for the fictitious name to keep receipts so that he can be reimbursed.
- Collect and record receipts from anyone spending money on behalf of the club.
- Identify who will call the IRS, or download from the Internet, the SS-4 form to apply for your club's Tax ID number.
- If you have a good turnout for this meeting, assign a small committee to work on your partnership agreement and your by-laws.
- Decide to join NAIC (National Association of Investors Corp.).
- Decide whether or not to have food at meetings and the type of refreshments.
- Decide on a date, time, and place for the next meeting.

Operating Action Items

- Have the leader state why he wants to start an investment club.
- Discuss the pros and cons of the different business structures for investment clubs and decide which type you will implement.

- Present potential names for the club, or start thinking of a name.
- Start thinking about how many members you want in the club, as well as the gender, minimum age, and geographic makeup of the membership.
- Get an idea of, or decide, how much it should cost to join the club: Start-up, Membership, and Monthly Investment fees.
- Select a commercial bank. Assign someone to check on opening a savings account and bring signature cards to Meeting # 2.

Follow-up Action Items

- Assign someone to compile a typed prospective membership list and bring to Meeting #2.
- Assign someone to draft a letter to send to additional people you wish to recruit. Include items about the club fees, and the next meeting date, time and location.
- Follow up with phone calls to the people being recruited.
- Assign someone to contact NAIC to get the Official Guide and Membership Guide.
- Schedule your next meeting for 2 to 3 weeks later.
- Assign someone to type up meeting minutes and bring copies for distribution at the next meeting.
- Prepare a typed meeting agenda.

CHAPTER 8

MEETING #2: PREPARE THE SOIL

Objective of Meeting #2:

To introduce the concepts, principles, and expectations of forming an investment club.

Housekeeping Action Items

- Recruit more members if necessary.
- Start the process for obtaining a Tax ID number, if not already done.
- If the name of the club is agreed on, ascertain if the name is available by having someone contact the Department of State, Division of Corporations, Fictitious Name Registration Department.

Administrative Action Items

- Have an introductory session (Meet & Greet).
- Learn why each member is there and what he or she expects from the club.
- Learn what everybody thinks he can contribute to the club.
- Learn what skills the new people have.
- Learn what equipment they have available (personally or through others).
- Decide who wants to come on board as a Charter member. Have each person who commits to being a part of the club complete the application form.

- Make the following assignments:
  - A temporary President, Secretary, Treasurer, and Historian.
  - A small committee to work on the bylaws and partnership agreement, if not done at Meeting #1.
  - People to attend NAIC meetings for Treasurers, for understanding the NAIC "Stock Selection Guide," and for the various computer groups.
  - Someone to obtain a copy of NAIC's *Better Investing* magazine.
  - Someone to compile a membership list from the application forms and make copies to hand out at the next meeting.
  - Open a joint savings account at a commercial bank. Collect the start-up fees. Give each person a receipt.
  - Set the date, time, and place of the next meeting, and set its time limit. Assign some one to prepare a typed agenda.

Operating Action Items

- Have one of the founding members conduct the meeting.
- Discuss and decide on a club name (if not done in Meeting #1).
- Discuss and decide on a permanent meeting place.
- Discuss the investment principles, risk tolerance, and overall club objectives.
- Make the final decision about the amount of the start-up and membership fees to be collected from each person joining the club.
- Make the final decision about the amount to be collected each month for investment purposes; make it affordable for all.
- Decide whether additional recruiting is needed, or whether enough members are already available.
- Decide on attendance requirements to remain a club member.
- Decide who will be signers on the club's savings account and complete the signature cards.
- Decide which two club officers will sign on the bank account; at least one of the signers should be your Treasurer.

Follow-up Action Items

- Set up a convenient mailing address for the club. We suggest using a post office box. Assign someone to be responsible for picking up the mail.
- If anyone has received a copy of the *NAIC Investor Manual*, assign someone to read the first chapter, and present a summary at the next meeting.
- Suggest members locate a copy of the *Wall Street Journal, Investors Business Daily*, or any of the financial magazines (all are available at your local library), and start browsing.
- Schedule the third meeting for 3 to 4 weeks later so you have enough time to get things done.
- It sounds like a lot, and it is. So the club remains fun and exciting for all, have each person take on an assignment or two, and present a report at Meeting # 3. This is one way to make sure everyone is part of the building process and no one person gets bogged down in the work.

CHAPTER 9

MEETING #3: PLANT THE SEEDS

Objective of Meeting # 3:

To establish the foundation, the objectives, the philosophy, and the membership of the club.

Housekeeping Action Items

- Have a printed agenda and distribute copies.
- Distribute copies of the membership list with complete addresses, e-mail, telephone, and fax numbers of all members.
- Have open and respectful discussions on all issues. These meetings are to establish your partnership.

Administrative Action Items

- Call the meeting to order.
- Welcome any new members, and again learn what they hope to get out of the club, their commitment, and their skills and resources.
- The temporary Secretary is to take notes. (See sample in the Appendix.)
- The temporary Treasurer is to give a status report. (See sample in the Appendix.)
- All people with an assignment are to report. Follow the agenda and set a time limit for the amount of discussion before moving on to the next report.
- Obtain status report from the Partnership/Bylaws committee.

- Begin researching brokers. Assign one or two people to call and compare broker fees and services, get application forms, and read about the NAIC Low Cost Investment Plan.

Operating Action Items

- Decide at this meeting on the initial value of a unit for investment.
- Decide if all members must put in the same amount each month for the first year. (Our recommendation is yes).
- Decide if there will be a fee assessed to members who miss meetings.
- Decide if members present agree that each is committed to stay in the club for at least one year.
- Decide if there is a penalty for withdrawing before one year from the date of joining. Some clubs include in their bylaws or partnership agreements that any member who withdraws from the club within a year of joining shall forfeit all investment monies, including fees.
- Decide what percentage of the club holdings a member may not exceed. You don't want any one member holding a controlling interest in the club.
- Decide if any withdrawal of monies will be allowed, and after how many years. Address the procedural details in your bylaws.
- Decide on the criteria for joining after this meeting.
- Decide whether to purchase NAIC's video on "How to Conduct a Meeting." Assign someone to complete the purchase and bring the video to the next meeting.
- Confirm the next meeting date, time, place, and items for the next agenda.

Follow-up Action Items

- Call NAIC to request, or download if available from the Internet, a Regional Chapter newsletter, and a calendar of events in your geographic area.
- Encourage members to attend NAIC workshops. Each member should commit to attend at least two workshops during this organizational period.

- Explore other investment options: the NAIC Low Cost Investment Plan, and Dividend Reinvestment Plans (DRIPS).
- Send out a reminder for the next meeting.
- Send a draft of the bylaws and partnership agreement to club members for their review prior to Meeting # 4.

CHAPTER 10

Meeting #4: Divide the Beds

Objective of Meeting # 4 :

To establish what approach the club wants to take to enter the stock market.

Housekeeping Action Items

- Get information on the NAIC low cost investment stock program as explained in the Better Investing. If you don't already have a copy, go to a council meeting in your area and get a copy; call NAIC or fax them to get contact numbers; or if you have access to the web use that method.
- Gather information on discount and on-line brokers.
- Copies of the draft bylaws and partnership agreement should be distributed to membership.

Administrative Action Items

- Review information on brokers.
- Review information on opening a money market account with the broker.
- Decide on a broker.
- Fill out necessary application forms and return to selected broker to establish this account as quickly as possible.
- Review NAIC Low Cost Investment program.
- Review past meetings for any leftover items and get them done.

- Start thinking about which 1 or 2 stocks the club might want to purchase.
- Decide who will make the stock purchases on behalf of the club.

Operating Action Items

- All members need to understand the function of a broker:
  - What information can the broker provide for your club?
  - What is the broker's role in the investment club?
- Decide what type of broker the club will use – discount, on-line, or full-service, and whether to invest in the NAIC low cost investment plan, other direct stock purchase plans, or some combination of these options.
- Work on bylaws and partnership agreement.

Follow-up Action

- Some members by now should be attending a workshop or two about investing.
- Identify members who will research online investing, if not done.
- Identify the member who will contact the brokers and do phone interviews with them.
- Find out the procedures for receiving and returning the broker applications.
- Make any additions to bylaws and partnership agreement.
- Review and revise the draft of the bylaws and partnership agreement
- Review what needs to be done for Meeting # 5.
- Send out reminder for next meeting.

Traveler, there is no path. Paths are made by walking.

Antonio Machado

Character is will, discipline, and the application of imagination to a purposeful goal.

Unknown

CHAPTER 11

Meeting #5: Tend the Crops

Objective of Meeting # 5:

To establish the club's operational and organizational framework.

Housekeeping Action Items

- If not already done, open a savings or checking account at a local commercial bank or credit union that charges no fees, or very low fees.
- By now everyone should have attended, or is scheduled to attend an educational workshop on stock analysis and selection.
- Do set a time limit - 3 to 4 hours. Be prepared! A lot of work will be done at this meeting.

Administrative Action Items

- Your club's investing rules:
  - Begin defining your investment philosophy.
  - Identify any companies you are opposed to investing in as a club.
  - Begin defining your investment strategy.
  - Determine your risk tolerance.
  - Decide how often you will make stock purchases - monthly, quarterly, etc.
  - Identify what criteria will be used to make investing or divesting decisions.

- Select the stock study tools the club will rely on.
- Decide if the club wants to become a member of the NAIC computer group, which studies and analyzes stocks via specialized computer programs.
- Decide if the club prefers to do the accounting and stock analysis manually or by computer.
- Decide whether to purchase the following computer software packages:

  - NAIC Club Accounting
  - Investors Tool Kit
  - Other Stock Analysis Program

- Order NAIC Club Accounting if you have not already done so. This accounting software makes it much easier for the Treasurer to manage the club's, and member's investments. Alternatively check out on-line club accounting options at www.naic-club.com.
- If purchased, view NAIC's videotape "How to Conduct a Meeting."
- Identify leader(s) for the educational sessions. Beanstalk has a three-person Education Committee that meets at least two weeks before the scheduled monthly investment meeting.
- Identify educational topics and start an education calendar. Schedule a topic for each meeting for the upcoming year. (See sample in Appendix)
- Vote on the broker the club will use and return the completed application.
- Assign the member who will contact and deal with the broker to set up a Money Market Account. (Usually the Treasurer does this but it can be done by any of the elected club officers).
- Plan for a field trip to your local library to get familiar with where the financial reference books and magazines are, and how to find them. (Look for the *Value Line* and *Standard & Poor* reports). We suggest you all go as a group. If you pre-arrange with the library, you may be able to get a guided tour of all the available resources they have to offer.
- Set the regularly scheduled meeting day and time.

Operating Action Items

- All members review and discuss a draft of your bylaws and your partnership agreement. Committee members take notes on revisions to include in the final documents.
- Hold club officer elections for the President, Vice President, Secretary, Treasurer, and Assistant Treasurer. Length of service should be limited according to your bylaws, such as one-year or two-year terms. It is a good idea to have understudies for these positions so that more members feel up to accepting these roles in the upcoming years.
- Appoint non-elected/committee positions.

Follow-up Action Items

- The Bylaws Committee and Partnership Agreement Committee finalize documents to present at next meeting for a vote.
- Education Committee should prepare the Education Calendar for distribution at the next meeting.
- By now, a number of members should have already attended NAIC's education workshops, steering committee meetings, and the Investor's College.
- If purchased, install stock analysis and club accounting software programs.
- Verify that the broker has received your application and opened your Money Market Account. To avoid problems with deposits, find out from the broker the correct payee that monthly investment checks should be made out to, and the account number. (*Note: the payee may not be your club, or the brokerage firm.*)
- Bring this payee information to your next meeting. This information should also be included in the meeting agenda.
- Process any reimbursements due to club members and distribute at the next meeting.
- Send out a meeting notice with the date, time, address, phone number, and directions to the library.

CHAPTER 12

MEETING #6: PULL THE WEEDS

Objective of Meeting # 6:

To provide an assessment of all the necessary building blocks to move on toward the last organizational meeting.

Housekeeping Action Items

- The club has a computer available loaded with the investment club software and members who know, or are becoming familiar with using it.
- All members know what a Value Line looks like.
- The club has on hand sample stock selection guides (SSGs)and the Stock Selection Guide video if members have chosen to do the stock analysis by the "pencil and paper method."
- The club has established a fixed meeting place for at least the next 6 months.
- Meetings are conducted in an orderly manner and according to minimum rules of order for voting.
- Pre-prepared agendas at every meeting.
- A treasurer's report is presented at each meeting.
- Meeting minutes typed and distributed to each member.
- Club owns video "How to conduct a meeting" and has viewed it
- Club owns Investors Tool Kit or other computer software to do stock analysis.
- Club has attained membership in NAIC and sent membership dues and a list of each member's name, address, social security # and their membership fee to NAIC.

- A copy of *Better Investing* is available, and the NAIC Club manual is available.
- Club accounting software is available and installed.
- The Partnership Agreement and bylaws are finalized.
- Several, if not all members of the club, have attended workshops on doing the SSG either manually or by computer.
- Some or all members have attended a computer workshop and participated in or observed how to use the computer analysis programs.
- Members are signed up for the NAIC Investors College, or some similar type of program at your local community college.
- Members are bringing in stock picks for study and review by reading the newspapers: *Investors Daily, Wall Street Journal, Barron's,* local daily paper.
- Members are reading magazines: *Money, Black Enterprise, Kiplinger's, Fortune, Variety, Women's Wear Daily,* trade papers, computer magazines.
- Members are listening to local and national money talk shows.
- Each member has visited the library and knows where to find *Value Line* References, both the *Value Line Index* and Reports, as well as *Standard & Poor's.*
- Club has a broker or a mechanism set up to purchase stocks: discount, on-line or the low cost investment plan.
- Banking issues are resolved or about to be.
- Club has a mailbox address.

Administrative Action Items

- Conduct meeting with agenda prepared from Housekeeping Action Items as listed here in Meeting #6.
- Discuss and resolve any stumbling blocks if you have not been able to accomplish all these items as set out here. The items are not listed in any particular order; however, each task should be completed.
- Select a Stock Education Committee and decide on a topic to present at the next meeting.

Operating Action Items

- Identify areas that need work.
- Identify members to get them done between this meeting and meeting # 7, if at all possible.
- Prepare agenda for Meeting # 7.
- Collect dues and deposit.

Follow-up Action Meeting

- Send out reminders for the next meeting.
- Delegate assignments for all so that all incomplete tasks are completed.
- Get to the Library if you have not done so.
- Stock Education Committee will meet and prepare presentation.
- The Historian should be prepared to take a group picture of the club at the next meeting to commemorate the beginning of your great adventure!

CHAPTER 13

MEETING #7: REAP WHAT YOU SOW

Objective of Meeting # 7:

> To conduct an investment club meeting using all the tools you have learned over the past several meetings.

Housekeeping Action Items

- Stock Education Committee has topic prepared for presentation.
- Members have attended NAIC or other suitable seminars.
- Members have received and read their NAIC manual.
- Minutes from the last meeting prepared for distribution.
- Broker and Money Market accounts have been set up.

Administrative Action Items

- Have a Value line for a stock, any stock.
- Ensure everyone knows where to find and how to find a stock in the *Value Line.*
- Have a newspaper available to look at stock prices and start reading the stock pages. Read all the symbols in the fine print at the bottom of the page.

Operating Action Items

- Call meeting to order.
- Present the minutes.
- Discuss any old business as noted in the minutes.
- Correct the minutes, if necessary, (something was reported incorrectly or wrong spelling of a name or word).

- Minutes are approved as amended by members.
- If minutes are approved, have them seconded and voted on by members.
- Call for new business
- Read treasurer's report: have that approved, seconded and accepted.
- Start your stock education.

Follow-up Action Items

- You made it. You are now a real live investment club.
- Each month you will study stocks, follow the investment principles and methods and invest.
- Remember the four aspects of your cornerstone:
   Respect.
   Tolerance.
   Trust.
   Kinship.

You are now on the exciting journey of INVESTING! From here on its all about reading, learning to use the tools, attending meetings, and making that first exciting call to a broker or placing your order on-line, and sending your money to BUY THAT VERY FIRST STOCK.

PART III

HOW TO KEEP YOUR CLUB GOING AND GROWING

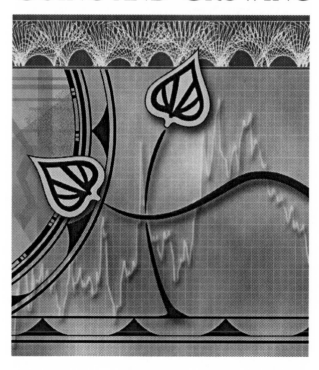

CHAPTER 14

ANNUAL HARVEST MEETING

Goals of Annual Harvest Meeting:

The goals of the Annual Meeting are to evaluate the performance of the portfolio, to determine if the club's objectives are aligned with the club's mission, and to plan for the future.

Housekeeping Action Items

- Set aside 3 to 4 hours for this annual meeting. Prepare an agenda. Assign someone to make the arrangements for the meeting area. Beanstalk's Annual Harvest Meeting is held each September, our anniversary month.
- Reward yourselves and make this a special meeting. Look for a special venue that is conducive to holding this type of meeting. Beanstalk has held our meeting in hotel conference rooms, restaurants, on board a cruise ship, and out-of-state.
- Invite a guest speaker to plant some new seeds of wisdom. Beanstalk does this each year, and we always leave recharged! We have had volunteers from NAIC, our discount broker, and a lawyer who discussed estate planning.
- Prepare an annual report. This may be done by one member who gathers all the information or by a committee. You decide. Be creative and present a well-prepared, professional, typed report to each member. Some sections to include:
  - Message from the President
  - Recap of the club's accomplishments

- Club's mission statement and objectives
- Investment strategy and stock selection criteria
- Club Portfolio Valuation Report
- Review of portfolio growth
- Analysis of investment diversification

- Bring a copy of your bylaws and any proposed amendments to the meeting.
- Bring a revised Partnership Agreement for signature by all club members, if necessary.

Administrative Action Items

- Have a fun icebreaker activity. We developed a stock jeopardy game some five years ago, and have had quizzes using the market's bear and bull symbols.
- Have a presentation from a guest speaker (optional).
- Review the portfolio's performance against your objectives and investment strategy.
- Establish next year's goals, objectives, and strategy.
- Confirm date and location of next meeting.

Operating Action Items

- Vote on any amendments to bylaws.
- Sign Partnership Agreement.
- Elect new club officers.
- Appoint committees and non-elected positions

Follow-up Action Items

- Get any additional signatures for the Partnership agreement.
- Prepare the Annual Education and Meeting Calendar.

We reap what we sow, the principle of the farm. It basically implies we need to do our homework instead of trying to "work the system."

If we put in the time and effort up front, instead of trying to find the easy way out, we will find things work better in the long run.

It is also a reference to planning and taking the long view.

Habits are powerful forces in our lives. They can hold us back, or keep us on course. They are consistent and unconscious patterns that allow us to express our character and produce our effectiveness or our ineffectiveness.

www.ryu.com/mascio/7 Habits

CHAPTER 15

INVESTMENT EDUCATION TOOLS

In This Chapter
- Trip to the Library
- NAIC Tools
- Stock Education Committee
- Mission Statement
- Investment, Buy and Exit Strategies

In this chapter we are going to discuss materials and methods that will guide you in studying companies.

Trip to the Library

If you have a company in mind that your club wants to buy stock in but have no idea how to access information or get a *Value Line* or *Standard & Poor's* Report, then start at the library. As Henry Ward Beecher said, "A library is not a luxury, but one of the necessities of life." You may feel a bit intimidated, but chin up, and either go directly to the reference section, or ask the librarian where the Value Line and Standard and Poor Reports are located. We are very much *Value Line* users.

Libraries have books, lots of them on financial topics. Beanstalk has held at least three meetings at the library so members could be aware of how to access the resource and reference material. Borrow books that teach you the simplest of things up to the most complex, remembering that complex is not complex once you have mastered it, and the simple is not simple when you do not know how. We remember borrowing books that told us exactly what a stock was, how to define Beta and so on.

Our primary resource for historical company data is the Value Line so let us walk you through that resource. *Value Line* has three sections:

1. The Value Line Index
2. The Value Line Investment Survey
3, The Value Line Selection & Opinion

When you find the Value Line Index and Investment Survey reports, you will find that there are two editions of each. The original reports track data for about 1700 companies. However, Value Line created a second set of reports that track an additional 1500 companies; so don't be frustrated if you don't see the company you are looking for. You may just need to look in the correct edition.

The Value Line Index lists all of the companies in alphabetical order, and is updated on a weekly basis. The index is a good place to start when looking for possible companies to invest in. You will find information on the current price, and other ranking statistics such as the P/E Ratio, beta, safety, timeliness, company, and industry ranking. Additionally, at the back of the index you will find several useful reports that list stocks based on several different investment criteria such as timely industries, dividend yield, and price appreciation. The *Index* will also list the page number where you will find the detailed report of a stock in the *Value Line Investment* Survey. Take the time to become familiar with this *Index*; it will save you a lot of time in your investment research.

The *Value Line Investment Survey* is divided into thirteen sections. Each Section contains detailed reports for the tracked stocks, grouped by industry. Each week one section is updated; therefore, an individual section is updated every thirteen weeks. The *Value Line Investment Survey* will give you a summary of the outlook for the industry, which is followed by one-page reports for each company. The reports will list from five to sixteen years of historical data, as well as analyst projections for the next three to five years. This is the report Beanstalk uses to complete the NAIC Stock Selection Guide for analysis of a company.

The *Value Line Opinion & Survey* gives you *Value Line's* forecast of the economy and the stock market, advice on investment policy, and in-depth analysis of stocks to consider now.

This report is also updated on a weekly basis, and provides a good base for understanding how economic conditions may impact current and future investments.

You can subscribe to the monthly *Value Line Reports*, and computerized stock screening software, however, we have found it more economical to just visit the library and photocopy the pages of the stocks we want to research.

NAIC Tools

Suppose you have no idea of what companies to research, refer to the *Better Investing* magazine by NAIC. It has features on Stocks to Study, Undervalued Stocks, free Investor Information Reports on 114 companies called Green Sheets, analysis of actual club portfolios, contact information for companies' Annual Reports, company advertisements, as well as at least 100 stocks listed which make up the NAIC Low Cost Investment program. These are all terrific places to start, and to continue to source your companies for study and purchase.

You will have decided whether your club is going to use the pencil-and-paper method to study. This will require getting the right stationary from NAIC and going to workshops to learn the technique for completing the tools and analyzing the information so that an investment decision is reached on the stock. Even if your club has decided to use a stock analysis software program, it is advisable for all club members to attend an educational session where the NAIC Stock Selection Guide is prepared manually. The understanding gained by actually completing the report yourself will be invaluable when applying judgment to the computer analysis.

Beanstalk uses the Investors Tool Kit computer program to prepare the Stock Selection Guides. Originally, the club had two approved software packages. The Tool Kit software provided us with more "hands on help," and it was certainly more user friendly. Regardless of whether it is paper and pencil, Tool Kit, or some other tool, it is the quality of the information and the judgment your club applies to the decision about a company's stock which will be of the greatest importance. The techniques and the judgment will come by regularly attending workshops.

You will learn that one piece of paper, be it a Value Line, *Standard & Poor's*, or an SSG is not the sole basis upon which a decision to purchase stock should be made. Information about the company, from a variety of sources carries equal importance. So the need to read magazines, such as *Money*, *Kiplinger's*, *Better Investing*, *Fortune*, *The Individual Investor*, and industry trade papers, is now a part of life. Read your daily newspaper's business section, the *Wall Street Journal* or *Barron's* if available. Listening to your local news money programs, as well as the national programs on money on Public Television and Radio, all provide information to help in making an informed decision.

Today research of any kind is accessible if not easier with the use of the Internet. Just don't download reams of information that you don't understand. Go slowly and work at it one step at a time. As you become clearer on the concepts, you can expand on what you take from the web.

Please understand that we don't endorse any particular resource, we are just trying to walk the walk with you, and share with you what has worked for the club. Having said that, we have found the following websites to be very useful:

NAIC's website www.better-investing.org, www.iclub.com, www.quicken.com, www.fool.com, www.excite.com, www.multexinvestor.com, www.blackenterprise.com, www.money-central.msn.com, www.smartmoney.com.

Join the NAIC computer group. Its publication BITS is an excellent resource for stock study. Attend a local, state, or national COMPUFEST which is the name given by NAIC to its computer seminars.

So how do you put all of this library visiting, listening to television, and observing trends in your community into a manageable format? Well obviously that is through the investment club you just started. But the real question is: "How do I really do it in the club?" There are books and programs specifically designed by NAIC such as The Investors College, or even fundamental financial courses at your local community college, which will take you step by step through analyzing your stocks. This is NOT that book.

Most of the local charter members of Beanstalk attended the Investors College and we recommend this highly. In our community, once a year, Phil Keating of the NAIC has a 3 hour workshop on Portfolio Management. Annually, either a member, or the entire membership, attends this workshop. For our first few years we barely came back with one concept, but we kept going back. In this seminar he analyzes portfolios submitted by clubs. We urge you to participate if your NAIC council has such a program. It is a great learning tool. One year our portfolio was honored as the #1 WINNING portfolio. It can happen to your club!!!!

Stock Education Committee

Within the club we established a stock education committee from among those members who seemed to have a good grasp of using the computer, as well as Pencil and Paper SSG preparation. The committee conducted additional education sessions for members, and prepared the computer SSG's for each meeting.

The downside of having a stock education committee is that members who are not actually doing the stock study may soon forget if they do not keep up with the fundamentals. To counteract this problem we tried assigning each member a stock. This worked in terms of information gathering on their stock, but again, as the members were not doing the SSG, some could not remember how to interpret the results.

We have now assigned industries to each member, and have made each person responsible for doing the SSG with the help of someone from the Stock Education committee. This is getting good results. As members realize how much they need to know, they are asking for and seeking more and more education! Each member needs to know how to complete an SSG and interpret it. This has to be an ongoing commitment of the club.

The major part of the club meeting should be dedicated to education about stocks and investing and the decision by vote as to what will be purchased or sold. If the stock presented is "good" meaning it meets whatever criteria the club has predetermined, but a decision not to purchase is made either due to lack of funds, or the price is not in the buy range, this stock goes on the Stock Watch List. (See Sample in the Appendix.)

Let's stop for a moment and summarize:

1. You want to form an investment club.
2. There are two to four founding members doing the ground-work.
3. You have ordered the NAIC Official Guide and Club Manual.
4. You are telling others about the club and inviting them to a meeting - date, time, and place have been decided.
5. You have named the club or have decided on a couple of names to present at the meeting.
6. You have either placed a notice in the community newspaper advertising the fictitious name, or you know how to go about it.
7. You have obtained a Tax ID number or are in the process of completing the task.
8. You have begun researching potential brokers.
9. You are gathering information and keeping receipts for the club's start-up costs.
10. You are having FUN!

As a bonus we have included the latest versions of Beanstalk's mission statement, investment strategy, buy strategy, and exit strategy. If put in place early, these guidelines will keep you focused and help keep you aware of when you might need to make a decision to sell.

Mission Statement

To make sound investment decisions through a commitment to educating ourselves about the investment world and following a principled investment strategy.

Investment Strategy

- Our goal is to maximize and realize the appreciation of our investments.
- We follow NAIC principles and guidelines
  - Review guidebook and other educational materials
  - Read Better Investing Magazine
  - Attend Investment Fairs and Education Seminars

- We are open to using all available tools to research and support our investment decisions
- We invest for the long term: 3-5 years
- We invest in aggressive growth companies
- We invest regularly
- We believe in portfolio diversification
- By industry/sector
    - By size/market capitalization
    - By asset allocation within the portfolio
- We maintain a mutual fund in our portfolio to provide investing flexibility
- Our target annual Rate of Return is 18%
- We review our portfolio regularly: quarterly
- We maintain a stock watch list to help to manage our portfolio.
- We maintain a standing Education committee whose purpose is:
    - To present prepared investment education topics
    - To generate the SSG, Challenge Tree, and PERT.

Buy Strategy

- Diversification: Research timely stocks in timely industries
    - Review industry performance and key success factors
    - Identify Industry leaders
    - Evaluate the company's strategic plan, what they do and how they do it, via articles, annual reports, 10K's, 10Q's, and Internet resources.
- Portfolio Asset Allocation and Market Capitalization:
    Small: 25%   Mid: 50%   Large: 25%
- Minimum holdings: 100 shares
- Preferred initial source: Value Line
    - Timeliness/Safety/Beta/Analysts growth projections
    - Review industry and company synopsis
    - Select challenge tree companies
- Assign stock to a club member to monitor and provide update to club.
- Education Committee Stock Analysis
    - Prepare Stock Selection Guide
    - Prepare Challenge Tree of comparative companies

- Prepare Stock Study Worksheets
- Present stock analysis to club for discussion and investment decision
- Investment Decision Criteria:
  (Based on Analysis Checklist by Phil J. Keating, CFA)
  - Growth & Profitability - How good is the company
  - Valuation - How inexpensive is the stock
  - Total Return and Yield - Appreciation and Dividends
  - Risk Management - Diversification & Financial Strength

Exit Strategy

When To Sell
(Based on article: www.individualinvestor.com)

- Reasons for owning the stock have changed or are no longer valid
- Portfolio asset allocation has been thrown way out of whack
- The stock or the fund has become too popular and too pricey (overvalued)
- The investment has been losing too much for too long
- The stock or the fund is under-performing its peer group
- Any capital gain can be offset with losses, or with a more profitable investment
- The company or the fund has unexpectedly changed management or strategy

Why Sell
- Valuation: Performance Vs Targets differ widely

What To Sell
- First: Sell the losers
- Second: Sell companies with falling earnings or which are in declining industries
- Third: Trailing sector averages in sales growth, net profit margin, or return on equity
- Fourth: Sell the winners - stock selected because it was undervalued is considered ripe for sale when it reaches its target valuation

The application of knowledge is power.

UNKNOWN

The only person who can predict the future is the one who creates it.

UNKNOWN

CHAPTER 16

IT'S BLOOMING FUN

IN THIS CHAPTER
- Keeping the Fun in Your Club
- Togetherness, Sharing, Learning
- Fruits of Success

Keeping the Fun in Your Club

There have been bumps in the road, but not too many we hope. All the preparation is done and you are ready for the real adventures of investing.

Whatever the reason people may have for wanting to join an investment club, all must feel committed and reach consensus about why they want to be in the club. All must feel that they want to work toward achieving the club's educational goals and financial success as part of the deal. This is the "All for One and One for All" bond of the immortalized "Three Musketeers." You have to be in this *together*. We cannot stress this point enough! To help you to achieve this level of excellence we offer the following tips:

- R.E.S.P.E.C.T - remember that song? That is what it is all about. Respect is the most precious ingredient as you begin investing.
- REVIEW - review and use the concepts of *The Investing Cycle©*. Follow NAIC principles of investing for the long term by diversifying your portfolio and investing in growth stocks.

- READ - the NAIC manual and attend seminars, call clubs, get help, give help. Every member should be reading the NAIC Investor Manual. There is much you will not understand at this point, but one day soon you will be able to decipher more and more of the hieroglyphics.
- PREPARE - do the homework of researching the stocks; prepare the SSG or your stock analysis before each monthly meeting, and study, study.
- ACCEPT - know that in any group there are those who will be more involved, and will work harder. Let it not be an issue. Find out what makes each club member tick and give each person assignments he will enjoy.
- CONCEDE - all members in the club are equals, each person carries one vote, and each person is to be heard. Never let meeting issues take place outside of the club's meetings. No one, two, three, or five people "own" the club.
- ENJOY - if learning and investing in this club is not fun it will not survive.

Togetherness, Sharing, Learning

The quality of your harvest is directly proportional to the level of effort you expend in executing the seven steps of *The Investing Cycle©*. In other words, you'll get out of it what you put into it.

When you invest your money in a mutual fund, you expect the fund manager to choose securities that will yield a consistent and significant return on your investment. Set your expectations as high as you would for any professional fund manager. To help you achieve this level of excellence we offer the following tips:

1. Making each person responsible for following one or two stocks or an industry is a good idea. Each Beanstalk member has two stocks and an industry that she follows. All club members, however, bring any information they have read or heard about any stock in the portfolio to the monthly meeting.

2. Present the price of the stocks in your portfolio at each meeting. A sample of the *__Stock Price Tracking Sheet__* that we use is included in the Appendix.

3. Establish a stock purchase schedule. Make purchasing stocks a regular part of your meetings. Some clubs make purchases monthly, while others save their monthly investments and make purchases quarterly. Investing regularly allows you to reap the benefits of dollar cost averaging; the principle being your funds will purchase more when the market is down, and less when the market is up. However, over the long term it has been consistently proven that your average cost will be lower than trying to time the market - not to mention saving the anxiety.

4. Reinvest any earnings, dividends, or capital gains. Take advantage of the beauty of compounding. Remember our earlier mistake and don't blow your harvest on socializing; rejuvenate your garden.

5. Establish the criteria you will use to make your buy, hold, and sell decisions. The key elements are included in the sample *Stock Study Worksheet* in the Appendix, and the Beanstalk strategies in the previous chapter.

6. Review historical growth and earnings; evaluate management's performance. In addition, Beanstalk prepares a Stock Selection Guide to determine if the stock is projected to meet our annual return cut-off.

7. To gain constructive feedback, take advantage of opportunities provided by your NAIC Local Chapter to have your portfolio evaluated. Each year Beanstalk submits its portfolio to the Southeast Florida Chapter Portfolio competition.

8. Encourage all members to attend the National Investor's Fair, Portfolio Management Seminars, and Regional Conferences. As many members as are able should attend these educational sessions. You will attend mini-workshops, seminars, and meet with representatives of numerous companies.

9. Mentor your new members. The members of the Education Committee should take responsibility for easing your new adventurers into the club and bringing them up to speed. Set up one-on-one or ad-hoc meetings if necessary.

10. Prepare a new member club information packet. Include the following plus any other pertinent information about your club:

- Copy of the Partnership Agreement
- Copy of the Bylaws
- Investment philosophy and Stock Selection Strategy
- Membership Contact, Club Officer, and Committee Lists
- Education Calendar
- Meeting schedule with dates, time, and locations
- Fee schedule and buy-in investment required

Fruits of Success

Well, we hope we have taken you on an easier journey to start a club than we had. Stick to it. It's fun, and you will learn so much. Become best friends with the library. Listen to the financial shows on TV and the radio. As you grow and *Learn to Earn*, share your knowledge with all the other folks out there who want to start an investment club. Become volunteers and join your NAIC Local Chapter. You have the tools, the garden is well laid out and planted, you have looked the giant straight in the eye and guess what—you came away victorious. It was not easy, but it wasn't so hard, either.

Please write and let us know how you did, we want to hear what went well, and what did not. We want to hear from you! Your comments are important to us.

Happy and profitable investing!
Your Story Begins Now!!!

PART IV

FAQ'S

CHAPTER 17

FREQUENTLY ASKED QUESTIONS

IN THIS CHAPTER
- Answers to Frequently Asked Questions about:
- Club Foundation – Basic Information
- Club Formation – How To Set Up the Investment club
- Club Finances – What are the costs involved
- Investing – Questions about Purchasing Stocks

FOUNDATION:

What is an investment club?

The U.S. Securities and Exchange Commission website, http://www.sec.gov, defines an investment club as follows:

An investment club is a group of people who pool their money to make investments. Usually, investment clubs are organized as partnerships and, after the members study different investments, the group decides to buy or sell based on a majority vote of the members. Club meetings may be educational and each member may actively participate in investment decisions.

What do I do first?

Find the right mix of people who want to form a club.

Can two people form a club?

Not really. The point is that you need sufficient numbers to have enough money to invest as the idea is not to put a lot of money at risk while you are learning about investing.

After you get an interested few together what do we do next?

Set up an organizational meeting and set about the task of naming your club.

Why is naming of the club so important?

It is important in order to obtain a Fictitious Name and a Tax I.D. number.

Should there be a formal club agreement?

Yes. As outlined in the manual of the National Association of Investors Corp., a partnership is "an association of two or more persons to carry on as co-owners of a business for profit." Included in the NAIC manual is a sample Partnership Agreement that addresses how the club will operate. Also, included in the Appendix to this *Guide* is a copy of Beanstalk's agreement. You may adapt these resources to the needs of your club.

If you organize your club as a Partnership, you will execute a Partnership Agreement. Make sure each club member has carefully read the agreement and agrees to abide by these club rules. Whenever a change in your membership occurs, you should amend your Partnership Agreement by preparing a revised agreement and securing each member's signature. If this is logistically impractical, you may want to have some type of sign-off issued to the new member indicating that he or she has read and agrees to abide by the agreement. Then at your Annual Meeting (or earlier if practical) present the revised Partnership Agreement for all members to sign.

What should we be doing to prepare for a club?

The founding members should establish the goals, objectives, and operating and investment philosophy of the proposed club. Contact the NAIC and order the NAIC Official Guide and the Membership Guide. You can contact the organization toll free by phone: 1-877-ASK-NAIC or 1-877-275-6242, by mail: NAIC P.O. Box 220, Royal Oak, Michigan, 48068 or visit the website www.better-investing.org.

Sign up for the Investor's College series, which will teach you how to find good investments and growth stocks, how to use the NAIC Stock Selection Guide (SSG), and how to recognize value. The Investor's College is a program offered by some local chapters.

Do all club members need to attend the Investor's College?

Yes. We believe that every club member, sometime within the first year of the club, should attend the Investor's College. NAIC will be your primary resource as you establish your club for stock analysis and computer workshops. There are some members who will "get it" right away. These people should become the internal teachers for the club to help everyone along. We also strongly recommend that annual education requirements be included in your bylaws.

Are there other events put on by NAIC?

Yes. The following are events often organized by local chapters: Regional Congress, Investor Fairs, and Compufest. The national office of the NAIC organizes the National Congress annually. Additional information is available through your area's Regional Chapter or via the NAIC website. These seminars will help you launch your club correctly. Local Chapter Directors will also present special topics to your club or combined clubs. There may be a charge.

Are there additional organizations or associations beside NAIC?

Yes. There are numerous resources with good tools geared specifically toward investment education and investment clubs. These include: the American Association of Individual Investors, on the internet at http://www.aaii.com, Yahoo Finance at http://www.yahoo.com, and the Motley Fool at http://www.fool.com.

FORMATION:

How do we choose a name for our club?

Be creative and ask for suggestions. Keep in mind that you want your name to reflect your objective. Have fun doing this. Let the imagination explode!

What is a fictitious name and how do we apply for one?

A fictitious name is the term applied to the name chosen for a formal partnership. As a partnership, you require a name. Registration requirements vary from state to state; therefore, to protect the chosen name of your partnership, contact your County Clerk's Office. You may also be required to publish your chosen name in the newspapers. Here are a few steps:

- Have your investment club's name ready. Choose a back-up name just in case the name you pick has already been used. In some communities the name verification can be done over the phone.
- Call your community newspaper (the rates are cheaper than for a city daily paper), and tell them you want to advertise a fictitious name. They will quote the advertising rate and in most cases supply the form.
- Complete the form, pay the money, and once the name has appeared in the paper the designated number of times without anyone else claiming the name, then …
  YOUR CLUB HAS A NAME!

Do we have to put an ad in the main daily paper?

If this is the only paper in town, yes.

How do we get a Tax ID number?

After deciding on a name for your club, look in the telephone book for your nearest IRS office. Call them, and inform them you wish to apply for a EIN (Employer Identification Number). Request an SS-4, Application for Employer Identification Number, or download it from the Internet. When the form arrives, complete it and return it to the IRS via mail, fax or other appropriate designated method. (See sample in Appendix.) The EIN number can be obtained instantly over the phone.

Your Tax ID number, or EIN, is like a Social Security number for your partnership. This is the number under which the IRS tracks each member's profits and losses on his club investment when he files his individual tax return each year.

What about taxes, and how do they work in an investment club?

The tax reporting year is from January to December. The club is required to submit a 1065, Annual Partnership Return, to the IRS. The Club Treasurer is responsible for ensuring that all documents are prepared. The individual club members receive a Schedule K-1 from the Treasurer that shows the worth of their investment in the club, and any profit or loss for the year. Show that form to the person who prepares your taxes. This information will be treated on the income tax return as either additional income or loss.

Do we need a member application form?

It is a good idea for a club to have each member complete an application form giving basic information for mailing purposes: name, address, phone, fax, and e-mail numbers. The form should also contain a space for naming a beneficiary. This is necessary should someone in the club die. A sample application form is included in the Appendix. The originals are kept by the Treasurer and a copy is kept by the President.

Where should the club meet?

As simple as this sounds, treat the selection of a meeting place with great care. Beanstalkers meet in each other's homes. The hosting club member serves a meal at the end of each of our meetings. Other clubs meet in church halls, boardrooms, condo meeting rooms, and libraries. Some offer coffee only, others may serve light refreshments. It is the group's call. If you have the opportunity to meet in a facility where there are computers, and it is free, safe and convenient, that location is worthy of consideration.

How often should the club meet?

Most clubs meet monthly on a specific date or day at a specific time, (e.g., the 3rd Saturday of the month at 2 PM).

How long should a meeting last?

Typically, meetings last between 1 1/2 and 2 hours.

Do we need to take notes or minutes?

Yes! You need to take notes or minutes of all decisions made in the meetings. A tape recorder is especially helpful if you are not experienced with taking minutes and participating in a meeting at the same time. Keep copies of the minutes in a permanent file, and have the Secretary bring one complete set of all minutes to each meeting for reference. Copies of the prior meetings' minutes should be distributed to each club member to review and approve.

What rules should we use to conduct the meeting?

Not all of us are familiar with the basic rules of conducting a simple meeting. While an investment club has a relatively informal meeting atmosphere, it does deal with money, and decisions are made about how that money is spent. There is a need, therefore, for order and proper voting procedures. If no one in the club knows parliamentary procedure, get a copy of the Roberts Rules of Order book for your meetings. Try a second-hand bookstore. You may want to select a Parliamentarian to be responsible for the order of the meeting until club members are familiar with the proper procedures.

Should we buy the video on how to conduct a club meeting from NAIC?

It can't hurt. If your club wants to make this investment be sure that the cost of this video, which is fairly inexpensive, is covered in your start-up fees.

What are bylaws?

Bylaws are the detailed and specific rules that govern your club. They are really simple sentences that determine what the club will do.

For example, your bylaws will specify the length of service of elected club officers. They will also address the "buy-in" or "buy-out" membership clauses, or what percentage of the club holdings a member may not exceed.

If there is someone who has experience with preparing bylaws, let him or her go for it. If not, do what Beanstalk did. Don't re-invent the wheel - get a copy from another club and adjust it to suit your needs until your members gain a better understanding of the club's operating procedures. As the club grows, you will determine how and when bylaws may be amended to reflect the individuality of your club.

What are some of the key positions in the club?

Most clubs have a President/Presiding Partner, Vice President/Assistant Presiding Partner, Secretary/Recording Partner, and a Treasurer/Financial Partner. Use these traditional titles or make up some fun titles of your own. The club needs leadership and direction. It needs someone who is willing to take minutes and handle correspondence, and it needs someone who is willing to handle the accounting. The club may also need someone who has access to a computer and knows how to use one, or is willing to learn to use one. You may have among your members a person who can conduct meetings according to simple parliamentary procedure.

When do we have a club?

Do you have your tax identification number? Has your club's fictitious name been advertised as required? Have you executed your Partnership Agreement? Do you have active members? Guess what? You now have an official investment club!

FINANCES:

Are there costs for starting an investment club?

Yes. Typically there are start-up costs to cover initial expenditures related to getting the club started; membership fees for ongoing administrative costs of operating the club (for example postage and copies); and the club members' monthly investment.

Are the start-up costs to join the club and the membership fees the same?

Start-up Costs: These are generally one-time fees that can include photocopies, obtaining the Fictitious Name, computer software and worksheets that will help do the club accounting and stock analysis, and educational videos.

Membership Fees: These are fees required for the club to join the NAIC as a club, NAIC individual membership fees, and any annual fees the club assesses each member. These funds will be used for the clubs ongoing administrative expenses.

What is an amount to consider for start-up costs?

There are several factors to consider: the number of people in the club to spread the cost among, whether you will purchase computer software for club accounting and stock analysis or use the pen and paper method (not recommended). There are no hard and fast rules for this. Set the fees to join the club initially at a dollar figure that is affordable and also meets the needs of the club. Figure between $75 and $200 per person.

How much money should we invest each month?

The monthly investment fee is very different from the start-up or membership fees. This fee is the amount each member is required to bring to the club each month so that stocks can be purchased. This money is to be used exclusively for the investment transactions of the club; IT IS NEVER TO BE MIXED WITH OTHER FUNDS. For most clubs, the amount of each member's monthly contribution is between $20 and $30. Some clubs, however, have a monthly investment as high as $100 per month or more. As the club grows, the monthly investment amount may be adjusted by an amendment to the club's bylaws.

What is a "unit"?

If your investment club were a company that sold stocks, a unit would be similar to a share of stock. Each time a member makes a monthly investment, she or he purchases a unit, or some fraction thereof, of the club. The number of units you own, multiplied by the value of the unit, determines your ownership value in the club. At the club's inception the value of one unit is usually equal to the monthly investment fee. As your portfolio grows, the value of a unit will fluctuate with the performance of the portfolio.

Can any one member put in more than the monthly investment?

Once a club decides on the monthly investment fee, if someone wants to invest more, he or she should do so on a unit basis. Note that once the club begins to invest, your unit valuation will vary from the monthly investment amount. We strongly suggest that for the first year each member buy the same number of units to ensure that all members maintain an equal value in the club.

Can one member own so many units that he controls the club?

The answer to this question will vary based on each club's bylaws. However, to prevent this situation from occurring, your bylaws should specifically state the largest percentage of the club portfolio that any member is allowed to own.

How do we open a bank account?

Initially go to a commercial bank with no fees on savings and checking accounts. Designate your club's President and Treasurer as the account holders, or perhaps two other members who have easy access to the bank for opening the account. When the savings account is opened, make it a requirement that there be two signatures for withdrawing funds. Typically, start-up and membership fees are deposited into this account. Maintain separate accounts for investment funds which should never be used for administrative or other expenses.

Is there another way we can "bank" our money?

The club can open a money market account with the brokerage firm that the club has selected to execute its trades. A money market account has check-writing privileges, although there may be a minimum amount for which a check may be written. The money market funds can be automatically withdrawn to make the stock purchases if the same brokerage firm is used for the money market account and stock trades. Typically, monthly Investment fees can be deposited into this account.

Do investment clubs have some way of protecting the club's funds?

There is a $25,000 bond that can be bought by the club through the NAIC. Alternatively, you can contact your insurance agent and purchase a Fidelity Bond. Beanstalk has never felt the need to have a bond. This, however, must be an individual club decision.

Is there any other insurance offered?

The membership fee paid to NAIC now covers liability insurance. For example, if someone sustains an injury during the course of a club meeting, this policy may be responsible for covering the incident.

What happens when members routinely do not come to meetings or pay dues?

Both of these situations should be addressed specifically in your club's bylaws. For example, the bylaws may state how many missed meetings constitute a potential for removal from the club, as well as the procedures for removal. The club may require written notice if a club member knows he/she is going to miss several meetings; however, the monthly investment is expected to be remitted to the club in a timely manner. The same process may apply for lack of payment of any dues or fees. Perhaps if dues are not paid for a period of 90 days the club will want to institute a series of escalating reminder letters that may also culminate in removal from the club.

What happens to the club when members resign, or leave the club involuntarily?

Again, in your bylaws, establish what costs, penalties, or forfeiture periods the club will attach to the withdrawing member. There are many ways to handle this "buy-out" event. Your club's procedures should be clearly defined in your bylaws. Some clubs buy out the club member with stock. More often though, the club will use its money market funds, or sell some of its stock to buy out the club member in cash.

Most clubs include in their bylaws a requirement for a formal letter of resignation. The member's valuation at the next monthly meeting, after receipt of this letter, is usually used to determine the buy-out amount owed. Additionally, in their bylaws, many clubs specify a 90-day lag period between the valuation and the issue of payment. This period allows your club to accumulate cash in its money market account to avoid having to sell stocks to make the payment. Be flexible for the rare emergency which a member may have.

INVESTING:

Now for the fun stuff. You're excited, rearing to go. You want the thrill of that first purchase. Great! But hold on just a bit; remember you are investing for the long term.

Like most clubs, yours will probably have a favorite stock you can't wait to purchase. You can officially purchase your first stock after you have your name registered, a tax identification number, and your broker - but most importantly - after you have done the legwork and analyzed the stocks in a systematic and principled manner. Keep club members' interests in mind; they will be more likely to research and analyze stocks that match their interests. If the stock meets your investment criteria, place it on your *Stock Watch List* until you are able to make a purchase. (See sample in Appendix.)

As beginning investors, you will buy stocks based upon how much you know at the time. That is why we use the phrase "Learn to Earn." Time and increased knowledge will improve the quality of your purchasing decisions.

How do we identify companies that we will not buy stock in?

Decide whether there are any companies that the members of the club are morally opposed to. On the other hand, some people feel that a club has a fiduciary responsibility to make money. Whether the club will purchase any of these stocks should be a club decision.

Should we purchase computer software?

Yes, as quickly as possible. Consider purchasing the NAIC Club Accounting and a Stock Analysis software package. Both of these programs eliminate many hours of manual calculations and record keeping.

Where do we find information on stocks?

Visit the library and ask at the reference desk where they keep the books with the following names: *Value Line, Standard & Poor's, and Morningstar.* Take a look at these, and become familiar with where they are. Look through financial magazines, newspapers, and the financial pages of your daily paper. Look at the news and other financial shows on television. **Stop and smell the roses**, look around your communities, and take note of businesses entering, expanding, or exiting your city. Ask yourself, where do I spend my money? Where are the long lines?

What is a portfolio?

That is the name given to the collection of stocks you buy. Think of it this way - in your closet each item of clothing you own collectively makes up your wardrobe. In the investment world each stock you own becomes a part of your portfolio.

In civilized countries of the world, the question is how to distribute most generally and equally the property of the world. As knowledge spreads wealth spreads.
- *RUTHERFORD B. HAYES*

An investment in knowledge still yields the best returns.
- *BENJAMIN FRANKLIN*

Rule No.1: Never lose money.
Rule No.2: Never forget rule No.1.
- *WARREN BUFFETT*

That is a good book which is opened with expectation and closed in profit.
- *AMOS BRONSON ALCOTT*

CHAPTER 18

MEET THE BEANSTALKERS

In This Chapter
- Background on the Club Formation
- Who We Are
- Lessons Learned

In 1982 one of the founding members read a brief article about investment clubs. She thought this sounded like a great idea, so she asked co-workers who were actively buying stocks about this idea. Most had never heard of an investment club, and suggested she just go get a broker. Some gave quick advice such as, "You must buy large blocks of stock." Disillusioned, she did not pursue the idea. She believed that starting an investment club was something that could not be done.

The whole idea of investing either by the investment club method or by going through a broker seemed as daunting as trying to climb Mt. Everest, but the desire was always there, and she kept talking about starting such a club. She never gave up. She continued to read articles about investment clubs in magazines and newspapers, and encouraged family members and friends to form such a club. We were aware of a couple of big-name brokers, but they intimidated us because we believed that you had to have enough money to buy a hundred shares of any stock. We were told we needed an accountant and a lawyer. We were also cautioned that in the event one of us should die, this might create problems legally for the club and especially for those people who had children.

So in the face of all of these dire warnings, we opted to start a social club instead! We saved a set amount of money each month and then treated ourselves to some form of desired entertainment. Would you believe that for eight years we were saving assiduously and spending quite extravagantly - and not investing a penny! That was our world. We knew how to spend, and spend well. We find it interesting that only three of the original members, Sonia Charles, Patricia Edwards, and Pearline Hamilton from the social club are now members of Beanstalk.

We were laboring under the misconception that investing was for the rich—people who had saved, earned big salaries, or inherited lots of money. Patricia Edwards, however never gave up on the idea that an investment club was a viable undertaking. She then met two other ladies who were excited about this idea. Finally, the right three people who shared the same vision with a "lets go for it" attitude were together, and the seed for Beanstalk was planted.

Who We Are

The Beanstalk Investment Club of Miami is an all-female club. It took eight years before our social club evolved into the Beanstalk Investment Club. How did this evolution come about? The three founding members, Patricia Edwards, Deborah Carattini, and Mary Ellen Pryor, were all nurses who worked as Case Managers working with patients with very serious or catastrophic illnesses. Their job brought them in contact with many companies. They started to observe trends such as high volume and sales, so they started to think that it would be a good idea to invest in these health industry companies. But at the time those thoughts were just dreams. They knew very little about personal investing, and they did not think they had enough money to enter the world of the stock market.

These three intrepid women would not let the sun set on their idea to form a club, so they met one Saturday afternoon in early September on a sunny patio in South Dade, Florida. The questions flowed: What to name the club? How much would it cost to join? How to explore legal issues? There would be no hard sell to recruit prospective members. You either wanted to join, or you did not.

The founders decided that the most important factor for success was to invite people who would get along very well together. If prospective members were enthusiastic and were not naysayers or the twenty-question suspicious types, they would be invited to the organizational meeting to form the investment club. By the conclusion of this auspicious meeting, the founders had settled on the proposed club name, membership fees, and the amount to be contributed each month by each member for stock purchases. An application form, and invitation letter were drafted.

The club's first organizational meeting of the Beanstalk Investment Club of Miami was held on September 21, 1991, with twelve people in attendance. They had found their additional investment adventurers.

Lessons Learned

The club took its name from the children's fairy tale "Jack and the Beanstalk." Mary Ellen Pryor, one of the three founding members and first President of the club, thought the imagery of the giant and the nimble Jack climbing infinite heights on the ever-growing beanstalk symbolized our entry into the world of investing.

Oh, we stumbled, we fumbled, and we made mistakes. Our naive questions remained unanswered; we felt lost. Sometimes we didn't even know there was a question that needed to be asked. None of the Charter Members knew anything about stock market terminology, none had used a stockbroker, and no one had been in an investment club before.

We were all women working at regular jobs, and needed our paychecks. Our education and careers did not make us any brighter or more knowledgeable about the world of investing. But we had what an investment club needs most: enthusiasm plus a ferocious need to learn about creating financial independence; a oneness of purpose; a healthy dose of respect for each other and each other's opinions; and a clear understanding that the club would probably not make us rich. However, the knowledge gained by studying and working at understanding how to invest could be used on an individual basis to change our outlook about money, and our ability to make investment decisions that could have very positive results for us personally.

As we write this, we are smiling. How could we not have known all these things? It now seems so simple, but it is only because we have learned so much and it is a part of each of us today. Everything has a process, and it is the little steps that make it easy. Unless someone takes the time to walk with you and not ignore you, you will waste precious time, creating barriers to your success, and you may become frustrated or even lose interest and quit.

This *Guide* is our way of being there for you when you make the statement, "I want to start an investment club and need to know how!"

Over the years we have been speakers at many investment clubs to help them get started so they would not have to expend so much energy with the "trial and error" drill. Through this *Guide* we want to provide you with basic but necessary tools so you, too, can start a successful club.

We firmly believe if the fundamentals and the foundation are sound at the beginning and done well, your club will be a sustaining and profitable venture. This *Guide* is for all the people who want to learn about money in an investment club setting, and have fun learning together in a group. This book is for you. We want to make your investment club start-up less traumatic than it was for us. We want to help you avoid some of the pitfalls.

Starting an investment club has nothing to do with how smart you are or how much money you have. "In Search of the Green: Starting Your Own Investment Club" contains the answers to the many questions you had about forming an investment club. We hope we have answered all these questions.

We have kept the club together, we feel, through activities such as the Annual Meeting, attending investments seminars as a club, having members attend the National Congress, celebrating achievements by taking a trip to New Orleans, having our own beanstalk caps, bags and watches with our logo, and mostly through sharing ourselves with new clubs, old clubs, local investment clubs' educational programs and just talking about how good it is being an investment club member! By sharing, we constantly learn from others. We then bring back new ideas and educational information to our club. SHARING, LISTENING and LEARNING keep us INVIGORATED. We make our Christmas Meetings a family gathering, and one year had red T-Shirts with our green beanstalk logo placed squarely on the front. One member even has a Beanstalk plate on the front of her car. All trips, special meetings, club mementos and other accessories are paid for by individual members.

Maintaining the club for many years requires even more hard work, creativity, spontaneity, and attention to your garden to keep it growing, so that it can produce fruitful harvests, not only to the current members, but for those yet to come.

PART V

APPENDIX

APPENDIX

Sample Forms

Glossary
143

Index
145

PARTNERSHIP AGREEMENT OF
THE BEANSTALK INVESTMENT CLUB OF MIAMI

This Agreement of Partnership, effective as of Saturday, January 29, 2000, by and between the undersigned, to wit:

xxxxxxxxxxxxxxx	xxxxxxxxxxxxxxx
xxxxxxxxxxxxxxx	xxxxxxxxxxxxxxx
xxxxxxxxxxxxxxx	xxxxxxxxxxxxxxx
xxxxxxxxxxxxxxx	xxxxxxxxxxxxxxx
xxxxxxxxxxxxxxx	xxxxxxxxxxxxxxx
xxxxxxxxxxxxxxx	xxxxxxxxxxxxxxx
xxxxxxxxxxxxxxx	xxxxxxxxxxxxxxx
xxxxxxxxxxxxxxx	xxxxxxxxxxxxxxx

NOW, THEREFORE, IT IS AGREED:

1. **Formation.** The undersigned hereby form a General Partnership in accordance with and subject to the laws of the State of Florida.

2. **Name.** The name of the partnership shall be BEANSTALK INVESTMENT CLUB OF MIAMI.

3. **Term.** The partnership began on October 1, 1991, and shall continue until December 31st of the same year and thereafter from year to year unless earlier terminated as hereinafter provided.

4. **PURPOSE.** THE ONLY PURPOSE OF THE PARTNERSHIP IS TO INVEST THE ASSETS OF THE PARTNERSHIP SOLELY IN STOCK, BONDS AND OTHER SECURITIES ("SECURITIES") FOR THE EDUCATION AND BENEFIT OF THE PARTNERS.

5. **Meetings.** Monthly meetings shall be held as determined by the partnership.

6. **Capital Contributions.** The partners may make capital contributions to the partnership on the date of each monthly meeting in such amounts as the partnership shall determine, provided, however, that no partner's capital account shall exceed twenty percent (20%) of the capital accounts of all the partners.

7. **Value of the Partnership.** The current value of the assets of the partnership, less the current value of the liabilities of the partnership (hereinafter referred to as "value of the partnership"),

shall be determined as of a regularly scheduled date and time ("valuation date"), preceding the date of each monthly meeting determined by the Club.

8. **Capital Accounts.** A capital account shall be maintained in the name of each partner. Any increase or decrease in the value of partnership on any valuation date shall be credited or debited, respectively, to each partner's capital account in proportion to the sum of all partner capital accounts on that date. Any other method of valuing each partner's capital account may be substituted for this method, provided the substituted method results in exactly the same valuation as previously provided herein. Each partner's capital contribution to, or capital withdrawal from, the partnership, shall be credited, or debited, respectively, to that partner's capital account.

9. **Management.** Each partner shall participate in the management and conduct of the affairs of the partnership in proportion to the value of his capital account. Except as otherwise determined, all decisions shall be made by the partners whose capital accounts total a majority of the value of the capital account of all the partners.

10. **Sharing of Profits and Losses.** Net profits and losses of the partnership shall inure to, and be borne by, the partners in proportion to the value of each of their capital accounts.

11. **Book of Accounts.** Books of Accounts of the transactions of the partnership shall be kept and at all times be available and open to inspection and examination by any partner.

12. **Annual Accounting.** Each calendar year, a full and complete account of the condition of the partnership shall be made to the partners.

13. **Bank Account.** The partnership may select a bank for the purpose of opening a bank account. Funds in the bank account shall be withdrawn by checks signed by a partner designated by the partnership.

14. **Broker Account.** None of the partners of this partnership shall be a broker. However, the partnership may select a broker and enter into such agreements with the broker as required for the purchase or sale of securities. Securities owned by the partnership shall be held in the partnership name unless another name shall be designated by the partnership.

Any corporation or transfer agent called upon to transfer any securities to, or from the name of the partnership shall be entitled to rely on instructions or assignments signed by any partner without inquiry as to the authority of the person(s) signing such instructions or assignments, or as to the validity of any transfer to or from the name of the partnership.

At the time of a transfer of securities, the corporation or transfer agent is entitled to assume (1) that the partnership is still in existence, and (2) that this Agreement is in full force and effect and has not been amended unless the corporation or transfer agent has received written notice to the contrary.

15. **No Compensation**. No partner shall be compensated for services rendered to the partnership, except reimbursement for expenses.

16. **Additional Partners**. Additional partners may be admitted at any time, upon the unanimous consent of all the partners, so long as the number of partners does not exceed twenty-five (25).

17. **Transfers to a Trust**. A partner may, after giving written notice to other partners, transfer his interest in the partnership to a revocable living trust of which he is the grantor and sole trustee.

18. **Removal of a Partner**. Any partner may be removed by agreement of the partners whose capital accounts total a majority of the value of all partners' capital accounts. Written notice of a meeting where removal of a partner is to be considered shall include a specific reference to this matter. The removal shall become effective upon payment of the value of the removed partner's capital account, which shall be in accordance with the provisions on full withdrawal of a partner noted in paragraphs 20 and 22. The vote action shall be treated as receipt of request for withdrawal.

19. **Termination of Partnership**. The partnership may be terminated by agreement of the partners whose capital accounts total a majority in value of the capital accounts of all the partners. Written notice of the meeting where termination of the partnership is to be considered shall include a specific reference to this matter. The partnership shall terminate upon a majority vote of all partners' capital accounts. Written notice of the decision to terminate the partnership shall be given to all the partners. Payment shall then be made of all the liabilities of the partnership and a final distribution of the remaining assets either in cash or in kind, shall promptly be made to the partners or their personal representatives in proportion to each partner's capital account.

20. **Voluntary Withdrawal (Partial or Full) of a Partner.** After five (5) years of participation in the Club, any partner may withdraw a part or all of the value of his capital account in the partnership and the partnership shall continue as a taxable entity. The partner withdrawing a portion or all of the value of his capital account shall give a minimum of thirty (30) days written notice of such intention to the President. Written notice shall be considered received as of the first meeting of the partnership at which it is presented. If written notice is received between meetings, it will be treated as received at the first following meeting.

   In making payment, the value of the partnership as set forth in the valuation statement prepared for the first meeting following the meeting at which the written notice is received from a partner requesting partial or full withdrawal will be used to determine the value of the partner's capital account.

   The partnership shall pay the partner who is withdrawing a portion or all of the value of his capital account in the partnership in accordance with paragraph 22 of this Agreement.

21. **Death or Incapacity of a Partner:** In the event of the death or incapacity of a partner (or the death or incapacity of the grantor and sole trustee of a revocable living trust, if such trust is a partner pursuant to Paragraph 17 hereof), receipt of notice of such an event shall be treated as notice of full withdrawal.

22. **Terms of Payment.** In the case of a partial payment (after five years of participation in the Club), it may be made in cash or securities or a mix of each at the option of the partner making the partial withdrawal. In the case of a full withdrawal, payment may be made in cash or securities or a mix of each at the option of the remaining partners. In either case, where securities are to be distributed, the remaining partners determine the securities.

   Where cash is transferred, the partnership shall transfer to the partner (or other appropriate entity) withdrawing a portion or all of his interest in the partnership, an amount equal to the lesser of (i) ninety-seven percent (97%) of the value of the capital account in the partnership being withdrawn, or (ii) the value of the capital account being withdrawn less the actual cost of the partnership selling securities to obtain cash to meet the withdrawal. The amount being withdrawn shall be paid within 10 days after the valuation date used in determining the withdrawal amount.

   If a partner withdrawing a portion or all of the value of his capital account in the partnership desires an immediate payment in cash, the partnership at its earliest convenience may pay eighty percent (80%) of the estimated value of his capital account and settle the balance in accordance with the valuation and payment procedures set forth in paragraphs 20 and 22.

When securities are transferred, the partnership shall select securities to transfer equal to the value of the capital account or a portion of the capital account being withdrawn (i.e. without a reduction for broker commission). Securities shall be transferred as of the date of the Club's valuation statement prepared to determine the value of that partner's capital account in the partnership. The Club's broker shall be advised that ownership of the securities has been transferred to the partner as of the valuation date used for the withdrawal.

23. **Forbidden Acts**. No Partner shall:

- Have the right or authority to bind or obligate the partnership to any extent whatsoever with regard to any matter outside the scope of the partnership purpose.
- Except as provided in paragraph 16, without the unanimous consent of all the other partners, assign, transfer, pledge, mortgage or sell all or part of his interest in the partnership to any other partner or other person whomsoever, or enter into any agreement as the result of which any person or persons not a partner shall become interested with him in the partnership.
- Purchase an investment for the partnership where less than the full purchase price is paid.
- Use the partnership name, credit or property for other than partnership purposes.
- Do any act detrimental to the interests of the partnership or which would make it impossible to carry on the purpose of the partnership.

This Agreement of Partnership shall be binding upon the respective heirs, executors, trustees, administrators and personal representatives of the partners. The partners have caused the Agreement of Partnership to be executed on the dates indicated below, effective as of the date indicated above.

BYLAWS OF BEANSTALK INVESTMENT
CLUB OF MIAMI

I. NAME
  A. The name of this investment club shall be "Beanstalk Investment Club Of Miami."

II. PURPOSE
  A. The purpose of the Beanstalk Investment Club shall be to increase club members' knowledge and information about investments, stock, and bonds and to invest monies monthly with the hope of future profits, if possible, and to have fun.

III. MEMBERSHIP
  A. The maximum number of members shall be 25.

  B. A simple majority of members in good standing may change the maximum number.

  C. New Member Selection:

    1. New members may be proposed and selected by a majority vote when a vacancy occurs. Upon joining, new members must resided in Dade, Broward or Palm Beach counties (tri-county area).

    2. Prospective members will be required to attend at least two (2) monthly club meetings and one (1) NAIC educational session prior to being considered for acceptance for membership in the club.

    3. Current active members in good standing will vote on a potential member's acceptance into the club, at a meeting to which the prospective candidate is not present.

  D. Monthly Investment:

    1. The amount of monthly investment shall be the minimum amount as established at the annual general meeting. It is due and payable each meeting date. Any member may contribute additional funds if desired, not to exceed an amount that is more than 20% of the club's current portfolio value.

    2. For the fiscal year, all members will be assessed an annual expense fee as established at the annual general meeting. Members have the option of paying the fee in four installments. The total amount of the annual expense fee must be paid in full on or before January 31st of the assessed year. This will become effective on October 1 of the assessed year.

  E. Failure to pay investment amounts due, without cause and proper notification shall constitute breach of membership. If not corrected within

30 days, said member shall forfeit membership privileges and be subject to buy-out, under the buy-out terms of the bylaws.

F. No withdrawal of funds by a club member will be allowed for the first 5 years of participation.

G. A member eligible to withdraw funds must submit a request to the President in writing a minimum of 30 days prior to the next club meeting. Such request should state the amount and date of withdrawal required.

IV. QUORUM

A. A quorum represents seven (7) members in good standing.

B. Members in good standing are eligible to vote. Payments of monthly investment amounts must be current to remain in good standing.

V. OFFICERS

A. Officers shall be elected at the annual meeting. They shall serve for a term of one year and may serve consecutive terms.

B. Officers and their duties are as follows and as stated in the NAIC manual:

1. President: Conducts meetings, fulfills and delegates other duties, as needed.

2. Vice President: Conducts meetings in the absence of the President, fulfills and delegates other duties, as needed.

3. Treasurer: Collects investment dues monthly; maintains Club's financial records; transacts all financial investments with stock brokers; files annual taxes as required by law.

4. Secretary: Records minutes of the club meetings: keeps membership informed of meetings.

VI. MEETING DATES

A. Monthly meetings shall be held on the 3rd Saturday of each month at a venue designated by the membership. The individual hosting the meeting will make a decision as to venue and refreshments.

B. Monthly meetings dates may be changed by quorum vote of those present at the previous meeting.

C. If monthly investment dues of $30.00 are not remitted by the Friday following the scheduled meeting date, a late charge of $10.00 shall be levied.

VII. BUY-IN/BUY-OUT

A. To buy out of the investment club, the valuation of the member's assets will be equal to the units in the account as of the postmark date on his or her letter of resignation. The person buying out is responsible for a payment of a 5% penalty fee of his pro-rated assets, to compensate the club for lost investment opportunities, commissions and costs involved. In the event of the death of a member, the beneficiary shall be assessed the commissions costs. Payment of monies owed to a member will be remitted within 90 days from the effective date of his or her resignation.

B. A member must submit his or her resignation in writing and forward it by U.S. mail to the club's secretary. The effective date of the resignation will be as of the postmark date. Should the postmark date fall on a weekend or a holiday, the valuation of the units in his account will be as of the last business day preceding the postmark date.

C. With the exception of the death of a member, voluntary and/or involuntary termination of a membership within one year of joining, will result in forfeiture of all monetary contributions made to Beanstalk, thereby excluding the new member from participation in Section VII A and VII B stated in the bylaws.

Form **SS-4**	**Application for Employer Identification Number**		EIN	
(Rev. December 2001) Department of the Treasury Internal Revenue Service	(For use by employers, corporations, partnerships, trusts, estates, churches, government agencies, Indian tribal entities, certain individuals, and others.) ▶ See separate instructions for each line. ▶ Keep a copy for your records.		OMB No. 1545-0003	

Type or print clearly.

1 Legal name of entity (or individual) for whom the EIN is being requested		
2 Trade name of business (if different from name on line 1)	**3** Executor, trustee, "care of" name	
4a Mailing address (room, apt., suite no. and street. or P.O. box)	**5a** Street address (if different) (Do not enter a P.O. box.)	
4b City, state, and ZIP code	**5b** City, state, and ZIP code	
6 County and state where principal business is located		
7a Name of principal officer, general partner, grantor, owner, or trustor	**7b** SSN, ITIN, or EIN	

8a Type of entity (check only one box)
- ☐ Sole proprietor (SSN) _____
- ☐ Partnership
- ☐ Corporation (enter form number to be filed) ▶ _____
- ☐ Personal service corp.
- ☐ Church or church-controlled organization
- ☐ Other nonprofit organization (specify) ▶ _____
- ☐ Other (specify) ▶

- ☐ Estate (SSN of decadent) _____
- ☐ Plan administrator (SSN) _____
- ☐ Trust (SSN of grantor) _____
- ☐ National Guard   ☐ State/local government
- ☐ Farmers' cooperative   ☐ Federal government/military
- ☐ REMIC   ☐ Indian tribal governments/enterprises
- Group Exemption Number (GEN) ▶ _____

8b If a corporation, name the state or foreign country (if applicable) where incorporated

State	Foreign country

9 **Reason for applying** (check only one box)
- ☐ Started new business (specify type) ▶ _____
- ☐ Hired employees (Check the box and see line 12.)
- ☐ Compliance with IRS withholding regulations
- ☐ Other (specify) ▶

- ☐ Banking purpose (specify purpose) ▶ _____
- ☐ Changed type of organization (specify new type) ▶ _____
- ☐ Purchased going business
- ☐ Created a trust (specify type) ▶ _____
- ☐ Created a pension plan (specify type) ▶ _____

10 Date business started or acquired (month, day, year)   **11** Closing month of accounting year

12 First date wages or annuities were paid or will be paid (month, day, year). **Note:** *If applicant is a withholding agent, enter date income will first be paid to nonresident alien. (month, day, year)* . . . . ▶

13 Highest number of employees expected in the next 12 months. **Note:** *If the applicant does not expect to have any employees during the period, enter "-0-."* . . . . ▶

Agricultural	Household	Other

14 Check **one** box that best describes the principal activity of your business.
- ☐ Construction   ☐ Rental & leasing   ☐ Transportation & warehousing
- ☐ Real estate   ☐ Manufacturing   ☐ Finance & insurance
- ☐ Health care & social assistance   ☐ Wholesale-agent/broker
- ☐ Accommodation & food service   ☐ Wholesale-other   ☐ Retail
- ☐ Other (specify)

15 Indicate principal line of merchandise sold; specific construction work done; products produced; or services provided.

16a Has the applicant ever applied for an employer identification number for this or any other business? . . . . . ☐ Yes   ☐ No
Note: *If "Yes," please complete lines 16b and 16c.*

16b If you checked "Yes" on line 16a, give applicant's legal name and trade name shown on prior application if different from line 1 or 2 above.
Legal name ▶   Trade name ▶

16c Approximate date when, and city and state where, the application was filed. Enter previous employer identification number if known.

Approximate date when filed (mo., day, year)	City and state where filed	Previous EIN

	Complete this section **only** if you want to authorize the named individual to receive the entity's EIN and answer questions about the completion of this form.	
Third Party Designee	Designee's name	Designee's telephone number (include area code) ( )
	Address and ZIP code	Designee's fax number (include area code) ( )

Under penalties of perjury, I declare that I have examined this application, and to the best of my knowledge and belief, it is true, correct, and complete.

Name and title (type or print clearly) ▶

Applicant's telephone number (include area code)
(   )

Signature ▶   Date ▶

Applicant's fax number (include area code)
(   )

For Privacy Act and Paperwork Reduction Act Notice, see separate instructions.   Cat. No. 16055N   Form **SS-4** (Rev. 12-2001)

The most recent version of this form (SS-4) is available at www.irs.gov.

☐ CORRECTED   ☐ PUBLICLY TRADED PARTNERSHIP

PARTNERSHIP'S name, street address, city, state, and ZIP code.	**1** Taxable income (loss) from passive activities	OMB No. 1545-1626	**Partner's Share of Income (Loss) From an Electing Large Partnership**
	2 Taxable income (loss) from other activities	20**03** Schedule K-1 (Form 1065-B)	
PARTNERSHIP'S Employer I.D. number	PARTNER'S identifying number	**3a** Total net capital gain (loss) from passive activities	**4a** Total net capital gain (loss) from other activities	**Copy A**
PARTNER'S name		**3b** Post-May 5, 2003 gain (loss) from passive activities	**4b** Post-May 5, 2003 gain (loss) from other activities	**For Internal Revenue Service Center** File with Form 1065-B.
Street address (including apt. no.)	**5** Net passive AMT adjustment	**6** Net other AMT adjustment	
City, state, and ZIP code	**7** General credits	**8** Low-income housing credit	For Paperwork Reduction Act Notice and instructions for completing this form, see the **2003 Instructions for Form 1065-B,** U.S. Return of Income for Electing Large Partnerships.
	9 Other		
Partner's share of liabilities: **a** Nonrecourse . . . . $ --------------- **b** Qualified nonrecourse financing . . . $ --------------- **c** Other . . . . $ --------------- Tax shelter registration number			

Schedule K-1 (Form 1065-B)   Cat. No. 25437H   Department of the Treasury - Internal Revenue Service

The most recent version of this form (1065) is available at www.irs.gov.

6511

Schedule K-1
(Form 1065)

2004

Department of the Treasury
Internal Revenue Service

Tax year beginning _____ , 2004
and ending _____ , 20___

Partner's Share of Income, Deductions, Credits, etc. ► See back of form and separate instructions.

☐ Final K-1   ☐ Amended K-1   OMB No. 1545-0099

Part III	Partner's Share of Current Year Income, Deductions, Credits, and Other Items

Part I	**Information About the Partnership**

A Partnership's employer identification number

B Partnership's name, address, city, state, and ZIP code

C IRS Center where partnership filed return

D ☐ Check if this is a publicly traded partnership (PTP)
E ☐ Tax shelter registration number, if any _____
F ☐ Check if Form 8271 is attached

Part II	**Information About the Partner**

G Partner's identifying number

H Partner's name, address, city, state, and ZIP code

I ☐ General partner or LLC member-manager   ☐ Limited partner or other LLC member

J ☐ Domestic partner   ☐ Foreign partner

K What type of entity is this partner? _____

L Partner's share of profit, loss, and capital:

	Beginning	Ending
Profit	%	%
Loss	%	%
Capital	%	%

M Partner's share of liabilities at year end:
Nonrecourse . . . . . . $_____
Qualified nonrecourse financing . . $_____
Recourse . . . . $_____

N Partner's capital account analysis:
Beginning capital account . . . $_____
Capital contributed during the year . $_____
Current year increase (decrease) . . $_____
Withdrawals & distributions . . $(_____)
Ending capital account . . . . $_____

☐ Tax basis ☐ GAAP ☐ Section 704(b) book
☐ Other (explain)

1	Ordinary business income (loss)	15	Credits & credit recapture
2	Net rental real estate income (loss)		
3	Other net rental income (loss)	16	Foreign transactions
4	Guaranteed payments		
5	Interest income		
6a	Ordinary dividends		
6b	Qualified dividends		
7	Royalties		
8	Net short-term capital gain (loss)		
9a	Net long-term capital gain (loss)	17	Alternative minimum tax (AMT) items
9b	Collectibles (28%) gain (loss)		
9c	Unrecaptured section 1250 gain		
10	Net section 1231 gain (loss)	18	Tax-exempt income and nondeductible expenses
11	Other income (loss)		
12	Section 179 deduction	19	Distributions
13	Other deductions		
		20	Other information
14	Self-employment earnings (loss)		

*See attached statement for additional information.

For IRS Use Only

For Privacy Act and Paperwork Reduction Act Notice, see Instructions for Form 1065.   Cat. No. 11394R   Schedule K-1 (Form 1065) 2004

The most recent version of this form (K-1) is available at www.irs.gov.

Annual Education & Meeting Calendar   Fiscal Year: _____

JANUARY	FEBRUARY	MARCH
*Industry Review: *Education Topic: *Stock Study: Admin Items: Distribute K-1's	*Industry Review: *Education Topic: *Stock Study: Admin Items:	*Industry Review: *Education Topic: *Stock Study: Admin Items: Qtrly Portfolio Review
APRIL	**MAY**	**JUNE**
*Industry Review: *Education Topic: *Stock Study: Admin Items:	*Industry Review: *Education Topic: *Stock Study: Admin Items:	*Industry Review: *Education Topic: *Stock Study: Admin Items: Qtrly Portfolio Review
JULY	**AUGUST**	**SEPTEMBER**
*Industry Review: *Education Topic: *Stock Study: Admin Items:	*Industry Review: *Education Topic: *Stock Study: Admin Items:	*Industry Review: *Education Topic: *Stock Study: Admin Items: Qtrly Portfolio Review
OCTOBER	**NOVEMBER**	**DECEMBER**
*Industry Review: *Education Topic: *Stock Study: Admin Items:	*Industry Review: *Education Topic: *Stock Study: Admin Items:	*Industry Review: *Education Topic: *Stock Study: Admin Items: Qtrly Portfolio Review

* Items should be scheduled for each monthly meeting.

APPLICATION FORM

_____

Last Name

_____

First Name   Middle Initial

_____

Street Address   Apt #

_____

City   State   Zip Code

_____

Home Phone   Work Phone

_____

Alternate: Cell/Pager

_____

E-mail Address

Beneficiary Information:

1. _____
  Name   Relationship   %

2. _____
  Name   Relationship   %

3. _____
  Name   Relationship   %

Application Form (continued)

_____

Why do you want to join this club?

_____

_____

_____

_____

_____

_____

_____

Initial Assessment

_____

Membership Dues

_____

Assessment Fees

_____

Club Mailing Address

_____

MEMBERSHIP RESOURCE LIST

Year: _____

Member Name Resources (i.e. computer, meeting rooms, photocopies)

Member Name	Resources (i.e. computer, meeting rooms,photocopies)

Meeting Agenda

I.   Meeting Called to Order: _____ (time)

II.   Acceptance of Prior Meeting Minutes: _____
                              (date of previous meeting)

III. Collection of Dues: $_____ (amount)

      Make checks payable to: _____

      Account Number: _____

IV.   Treasurer's Report

V.   Old Business
      A. Current Portfolio
            1. Stock Reports by members
            2. Stock Watch Updates
      B. Other Old Business

VI.   New Business
      A. Industry Report
      B. Stock Study Report
      C. Stock Watch Additions
      D. Stock Purchases
      E. Other New Business

VII. Education Topic

VIII. Roundtable: Open Discussion

IX.   Items For Next Meeting
      A. Industry Report
      B. Education Topic
      C. Guest Speaker (if applicable)
      D. Date, Time, Location of next meeting

X.   Adjournment: _____ (time)

MEETING MINUTES

Beanstalk Investment Club
November 18, 2004

Present were: [list the names of all present]
Absent: [list the names of all not present]

The meeting was called to order at 2pm.

MINUTES:
The minutes of the October meeting were read and approved without corrections.

OLD BUSINESS:
The group discussed and voted on the amendments to the bylaws as proposed in the October meeting. All amendments to section III Membership were unanimously approved.

TREASURER'S REPORT
• The treasurer collected all the dues. There are no outstanding or late dues.
• 50 shares of HCR were sold at $31 1/8.
• The following stocks were purchased:
   Home Depot (20) shares at $43.38.
   Southwest Air (10) shares at $ 14.50.
• Current Portfolio value: $78,000.
• Current account balances in Money Market Account: $150.00.
• Current Amount in checking account at [bank]: $250.00.
• Individual evaluation statements were distributed to each member.

STOCK EDUCATION
• The current prices for all the stocks in the portfolio were presented by Pat. Current updates on stocks in the portfolio was presented by each member.
• Lisa [education designee] went through the portfolio and our portfolio is over weighted in consumer staples. We own both COKE and PEPSICO. They are both in the same industry. It seems that we should sell COKE. The club will do an SSG on both and a decision will be made at the next meeting regarding which will be sold. The club will then decide whether to take that money and buy more Pepsi, or to put the money into a sector where we have no holdings - Energy.

• An SSG was presented on Bed Bath & Beyond. The front of the SSG has good straight lines. Evaluating management on the SSG shows that the trends are UP. The upside downside ratio is 3:1. The relative value is 102. The total return is 19%. In this sector, this is the number one company, though sales are not as high as in previous years. The number 2 competitor is Linen's and Things. The club voted to buy (20) shares of Bed Bath & Beyond.

HOSPITALITY
Cards were sent to [who is sick, graduated, bereaved, celebrating a birthday]

NEW BUSINESS
• The club discussed the need to purchase an upgrade for computer software. The club decided that the Treasurer should purchase the new upgrade.
• Club members were advised of ongoing educational workshops and seminars being conducted by the local South East Florida Chapter. Sonia agreed to attend the PERT (Portfolio Evaluation Review Technique) workshop. She will report to the club.
• We discussed that one member should read the BI thoroughly and report highlights to the club at each meeting. This was agreed upon unanimoulsy. Dee agreed to take on that assignment.

NEXT STOCK STUDY
The stock to study for the next meeting will be: COKE & PEPSI and each member is to research an Energy stock.

NEXT MEETING, TIME AND DATE
The next meeting will be at Mary's house on December 10, 2004 at 2pm.

ADJOURN at 4pm

Respectfully submitted by Mary E. Pryor

The minutes are strictly a guideline. We used these minutes to stress the importance of doing the real business of the club – education. In the early days the minutes will reflect the activities that you undertake to form the club, such as approval for your name, your Tax ID number, the setting of the bylaws and so forth.

STOCK STUDY WORKSHEET

Stock Name: _____

Stock Symbol: _____ Exchange: _____

Address: _____

_____

_____

CEO: _____ COO: _____

CFO: _____

Brief Description: _____

_____

_____

Stock Selection Guide Statistics:

Est. High Price (5yrs): $ _____ Est. Low Price (5yrs): $ _____

Buy Range: _____ Hold Range: _____ Sell Range: _____

Upside/Downside Ratio: ___ to 1   Est. Annual Return: ___ %

Target Appreciation: ___ %

Current P/E: _____ Avg. P/E last 5 yrs: _____

                                Avg. Industry P/E: _____

Current Price: _____

52-Wk High: _____ 52-Wk Low: _____

Timeliness: _____ Safety: _____

BETA: _____

Value Line Rating: _____ Standard & Poor Rating: _____

Market Capitalization: _____

% Insiders: _____ % Institutional: _____

Long Term Debt: _____

Reviewed: ☐ 10-K   ☐ 10-Q   ☐ Annual Report

Stock Study Worksheet (continued)

Financial Highlights:

Have sales increased steadily for the past 5 years? ☐ Yes ☐ No

If not, why? _____

_____

_____

Have earnings increase steadily for the past 5 years? ☐ Yes ☐ No

If not, why? _____

_____

_____

Are sales and earnings projected to increase in the next 5 years? ☐ Yes ☐ No

If so, by how much? _____

Sales: _____ % increase

Earnings: _____ % increase

Comments: _____

_____

Reasons to purchase stock: _____

_____

Action Taken: ☐ Buy ☐ Sell ☐ Hold

Date: _____

_____ Votes to hold for future consideration

_____ Votes to purchase / sell _____ shares @ _____ (price)

_____ Votes not to purchase / sell this stock

Member Stock Assignment: _____

_____

Prepared by: _____

Date: _____

STOCK PRICE TRACKING SHEET   YEAR: _____

Symbol	Name	Exchange	JAN	FEB	MAR	APR	MAY	JUN	JUL	AUG	SEP	OCT	NOV	DEC

STOCK WATCH LIST   FISCAL YEAR:_____

Symbol	Name	Exchange	Dom/ For	Last SSG Date	Return %	U/D Ratio	Buying Range	P/E	BETA	Industry Rank	Assigned to	Purch Price	Purch Date	/#

TREASURER'S REPORT

CASH ON HAND:

SAVINGS ACCOUNT BALANCE: $ _____

MONEY MARKET ACCOUNT: $ _____

TOTAL MONTHLY INVESTMENT OUTSTANDING: $ _____

_____

_____

TOTAL MEMBERSHIP FEES OUTSTANDING: $ _____

_____

_____

STOCK PURCHASES:

Name	Date	Price
Name	Date	Price
Name	Date	Price
Name	Date	Price
Name	Date	Price
Name	Date	Price

Treasurer's Report (continued)

Name	Date	Price

Name	Date	Price

Name	Date	Price

Name	Date	Price

Name	Date	Price

Operating Budget Category:	Budget:	Y-T-D Expense:	Balance:
Budget: Y-T-D Expense: Balance: Postage Office Supplies Printing & Stationery Film & Processing Videos Computer Software Books Dues & Subscriptions Annual Report Prep Other: Other:			

Prepared By: _____   Date: _____

GLOSSARY

Beneficiary - the person or persons named to receive your benefits after you die.

Mutual fund - a company where many people's investments are pooled and managed by professional money managers.

Portfolio - all the stocks which have been purchased and are currently owned by the club.

Stock - an instrument that indicates that you have ownership in a corporation.

Stock broker - a person who has the authority to handle the public's request to buy or sell stocks, bonds, mutual funds, etc.

Stock market - consider this as the forum where investment instruments such as stocks are traded, meaning bought or sold.

Stock Selection Guide/SSG - a form which when completed has numerical information which can be analyzed to determine if a company is a quality company and whether you might want to consider buying stock in that company.

INDEX

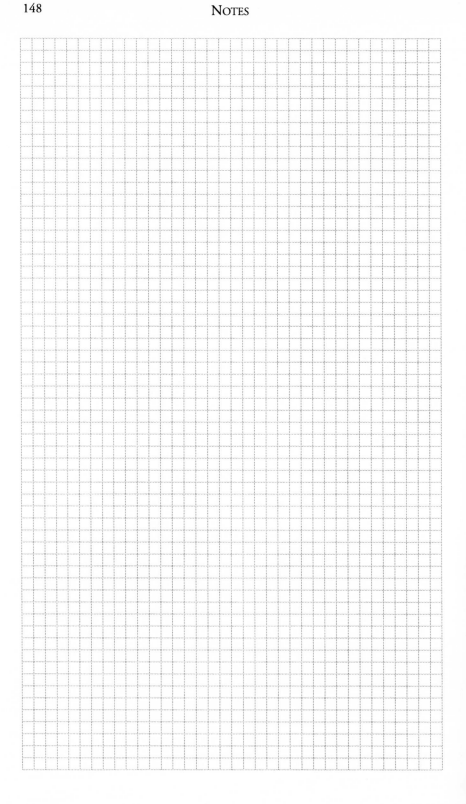

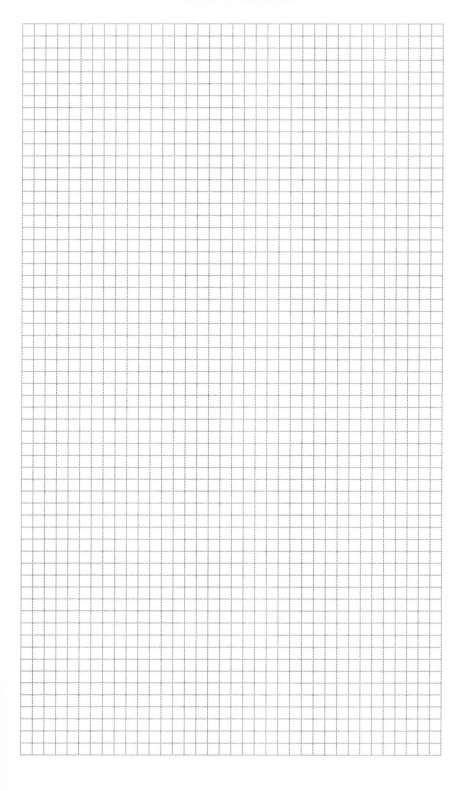

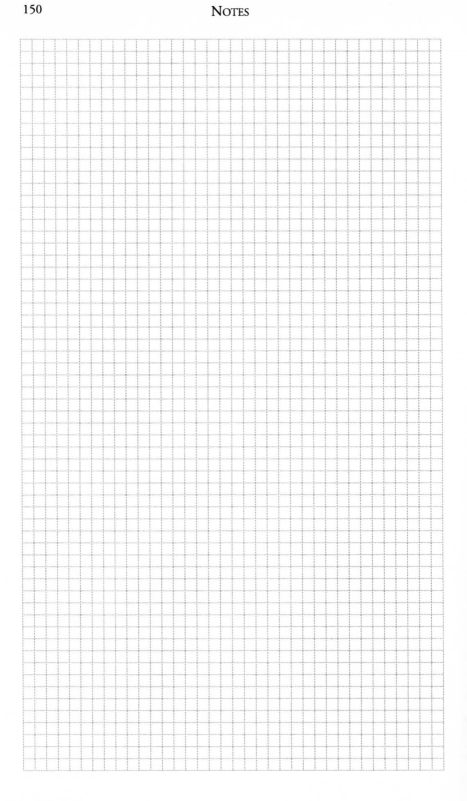

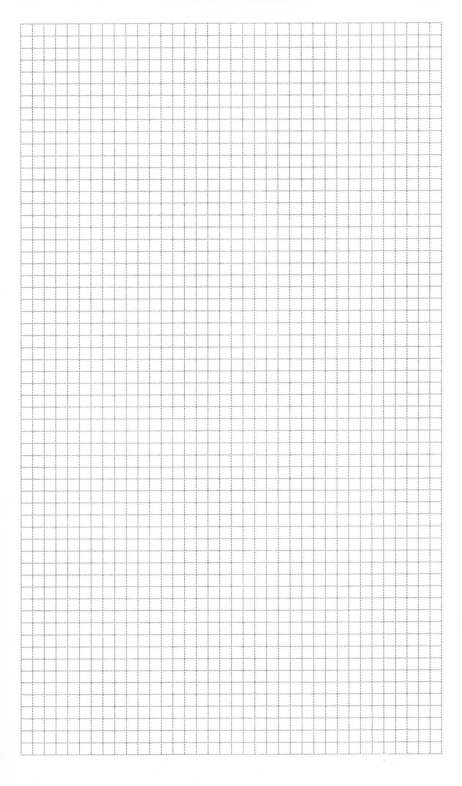

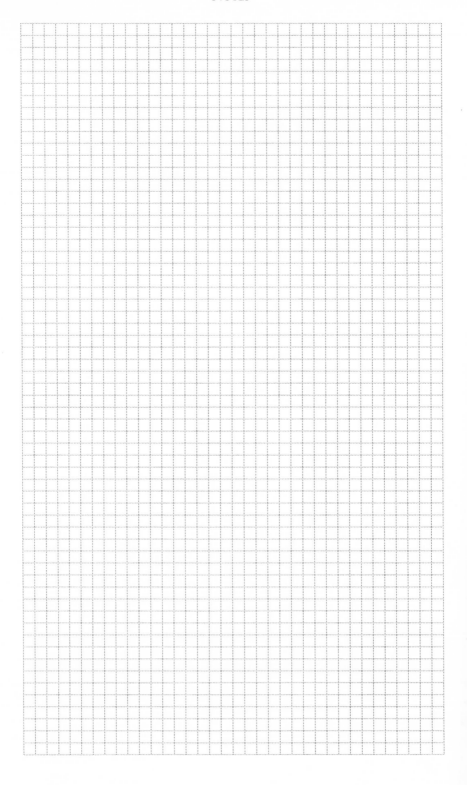

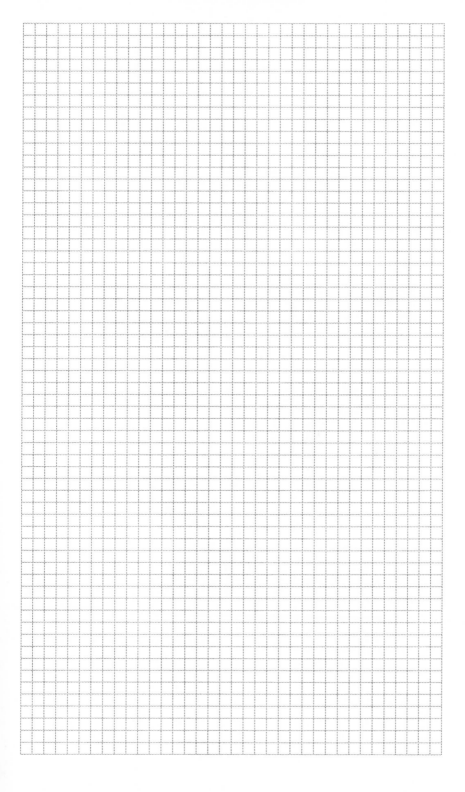

Printed in the United States
69697LV00003B/163

9 781420 873474